T0302647

THE POETS' GUIDE
TO ECONOMICS

THE

POETS'

GUIDE TO
ECONOMICS

JOHN RAMSDEN

 PALLAS
ATHENE

First published 2022 by
Pallas Athene (Publishers) Ltd,
2 Birch Close, London N19 5XD

ISBN 978 1 84368 221 9

Printed in England

CONTENTS

FOR JANE

Who made these pages possible

INTRODUCTION

If the great economists wrote poetry, they must have kept it private. The reverse is not so true. Coleridge gave us *Vulgar Errors Respecting Taxes and Taxation*. Ezra Pound wrote *The ABC of Economics*. Hilaire Belloc produced *Economics for Helen*. Walter Scott saved the Scottish pound note – his image has adorned it ever since. Jonathan Swift fought to save Ireland from punitive trade restrictions. For some, economic writing was a brief detour; for others, like Defoe, an obsession. Some absorbed the subject from newspapers and pundits, others studied it seriously. De Quincey, in *Recollections of the Lake Poets,* tells us that:

> Coleridge did not, like Wordsworth, dismiss political economy from his notice disdainfully, as a puerile tissue of truisms or of falsehood not less obvious, but actually addressed himself to the subject; fancied he had made discoveries in the science; and even promised us a systematic work on its whole compass.

Bernard Shaw studied the subject in the reading room of the British Museum (like Marx) and later co-founded the London School of Economics. Most of them found the new discipline both fascinating – for its grip on the public mind – and repelling. They had no time for economists and felt they could do better. John Ruskin was not shy of saying so:

> The following pages contain, I believe, the first accurate analysis of the laws of Political Economy which has been published in England.
>
> *Munera Pulveris,* 1872

Poets down the ages had treated money with lofty disdain. This was possible while the economy slumbered in its lair. Things began to change in Britain around 1700, with the birth of a modern financial system. By 1800 the industrial revolution was in full swing, an upheaval that changed the face of the earth. Ancient communities were swept aside. The misery of the 'dark satanic mills' needs no rehearsing. 'Political economy' provided the intellectual framework for this momentous process. Poets, who saw themselves as the guardians of civilisation, the heirs to Homer, Dante and Milton, could not ignore the challenge. They began to engage more seriously with the world of money and to offer their own thoughts on political economy. This book is an introduction to their efforts, beginning with Daniel Defoe in the 1690s, and ending with Ezra Pound in 1944.

Political economy underwent its own revolution. In *The Wealth of Nations* (1776) Adam Smith laid the foundations of modern economic thought. He showed how the self-interested behaviour of individuals, guided by a free market, could work to the benefit of the whole community. In place of gold, Smith made labour the true measure of value and productive investment the driver of growth. His successors, notably David Ricardo, built classical economics on this foundation. Smith's profound but much qualified insights evolved into a tower of logic, erected on shaky assumptions and a dose of metaphysics. Classical economics seemed to explain what was happening. Its programme of laissez-faire, free trade and sound money helped usher in a period of economic growth without parallel in history. But it was a brutal process, which political economy appeared to condone. Findings such as the 'Iron Law of Wages' —the idea that wages could never rise above a basic subsistence level — soon earned the title of 'the dismal science'.

Then as now, most people got their economics secondhand, from pundits and the press. The resulting brew accentuated all that was hard-nosed. Adam Smith and J. S. Mill were both philosophers before they turned to economics. Both disapproved of unearned incomes, large landed estates and business lobby groups. But none of these views found their way into what Walter Bagehot*

* Writer on the Constitution and editor of *The Economist* from 1861-78.

later called the 'common sense of the nation'. This was the 'common sense' that fought tooth and nail against shorter working hours for children. Coleridge railed against such thinking, as he campaigned for the first Factory Act of 1819. It was not just the cruelties but also the corrosive effect on culture that so alarmed the poets. As Bernard Shaw put it, in a centenary lecture on Ruskin :

> Ruskin, beginning as an artist with an interest in art – exactly as I did myself, by the way – was inevitably driven back to economics, and to the conviction that your art would never come right while your economics were wrong.

Modern economists come with Nobel prizes and great prestige. Their mysteries are conducted in mathematics, well beyond the reach of the laity. In Coleridge or Ruskin's day, the subject involved no maths and could be taken in from a handful of books. Its very name, 'political economy', suggested a field based on common experience. A poet could nail his theses to the cathedral door of political economy and expect to be taken seriously. It was society's unspoken religion – and it was breaking down. As unemployment soared and millions hungered, despair drove many into the arms of fascism or communism. Economics had no answers until Keynes, in the 1930s, finally worked out how to end the Great Depression. In doing so, he demolished beliefs which had reigned for a century. How, he asked, had the classical system lasted so long?

That it reached conclusions quite different from what the ordinary person would expect, added, I suppose, to its intellectual prestige. That its teaching, translated into practice, was austere and often unpalatable, lent it virtue. That it was adapted to carry a vast and consistent logical superstructure, gave it beauty. That it could explain much social injustice and apparent cruelty as an inevitable incident in the scheme of progress, and the attempt to change such things as likely on the whole to do more harm than good, commended it to authority. That it afforded a measure of justification to the free activities of the individual capitalist, attracted to it the support of the dominant social force behind authority.

The General Theory of Employment,
Interest and Money, 1936

The poets had been saying this all along. They knew that economics was philosophically flawed. It rested on a narrow, transactional view of human behaviour, at odds with real life. It proposed a model for society without an ethical basis – no good could come of this. The economist's notions of 'wealth' and 'value' were also wrong. Ruskin saw that things could have a market value, yet be the opposite of 'wealth' and leave us worse off in practice. There was scorn, too, for the economist's image of things smoothly 'adjusting' to a new 'equilibrium'. As Coleridge put it:

> We shall perhaps be told too that … all things find
> their level … but persons are not things – but man
> does not find his level! After hard and calamitous
> season, during which the thousand wheels of some
> vast manufactory had remained silent as a frozen
> water-fall, be it that plenty has returned and that
> trade has once more become brisk and stirring: go
> ask the overseer, and question the parish doctor,
> whether the workman's health and temperance …
> have found their level again.
>
> *A Lay Sermon,* 1817

These philosophical flaws suggested that political
economy must also be wrong scientifically. Economics
claims to be about the efficient allocation of scarce re-
sources. The poets looked around and saw perhaps the
most wasteful society there had ever been. Economists
said resources were best allocated by the play of demand
and supply in freely competitive markets. The poets saw
a gross misallocation of resources, due to extremes of ine-
quality which markets mirrored and usually made worse:
Bernard Shaw's society lady, ordering a luxury coffin for
her dog while an urchin starves in the street below.

Money was a case in point. Classical economists saw it
as a sort of veil, with no effect on the underlying transac-
tions. Poets knew that money was a force in its own right.
Credit was Defoe's 'coy mistress', mighty but flighty. Col-
eridge described the excesses of the credit cycle – what he
called 'Icarian credit' – and its effect on the real economy

of goods and services. Shelley thought finance squeezed out the poor; he campaigned to abolish the national debt and the paper currency. Scott fought for a banking system as accessible to a highland villager as a city merchant. Belloc expected a cataclysmic showdown between finance and the rest of society. They all warned, again and again, that finance unbridled was a menace. The financial crash of 2007-2008 would not have surprised them as it did the experts.

The poets were surely right about the excesses and limitations of markets, right to put humanity over economic dogma. But when this led them to reject market mechanisms altogether, they went badly wrong. Some looked backwards to a medieval guild system, others forward to a communist utopia. Either way, most had no time for parliamentary democracy. In 1944 Ezra Pound was holed up in fascist Italy writing tracts about usury, even as Allied troops fought their way up the peninsula, carrying a warrant for his arrest. Meanwhile, Keynes was planning the post-war economic system that led to thirty years of growth and full employment.

I have restricted myself to eleven poets who also wrote on economic matters. They are, alas, all men.* Were these eleven all poets? With Shelley, Coleridge, Scott or Pound

---

* Harriet Martineau popularised utilitarian theories in simple parables but was not a poet; Elizabeth Barrett Browning wrote moving poems about child labour but not economic pamphlets. Women poets do not seem to have moonlighted as economists.

the case is clear. Defoe and Swift are world famous for
their novels but were also prolific writers in verse. Morris
was invited to become poet laureate on the strength of his
verse sagas. Belloc's verse is (or was) familiar to every child.
Ruskin was a master of the prose poem, a bardic figure
who mesmerised his readers. De Quincey, a poet *manqué*,
is inseparable from the Lake Poets; his *Confessions of an
English Opium Eater* surely earns him inclusion. Bernard
Shaw is perhaps the borderline case, but he achieved almost
Tolstoyan fame in his day and won the Nobel prize for
literature. In any case, Shelley tells us that poetry can take
many forms and that:

> The distinction between poets and prose writers is
> a vulgar error.

There are brilliant biographies and a mountain of
scholarship on most of these writers. What follows is a
rapid dip into a small corner of their work. I may well
have over-simplified here and there: *mea culpa*. This work
is meant as a sort of guided anthology, with just enough
comment and context to make sense (I hope) of the ex-
tracts.

Economics matter. Bad policies, based on mistaken
theories, led to an economic collapse at the end of the
1920s. This set the scene for world-wide conflict in the
1930s. Will today's economists make a better fist of the
2020s? The years of Keynesian plenty are long gone. Eco-
nomics seems to be in trouble – too entrenched to be

stormed from outside, too narrow to cope on its own. A spate of recent books suggest that prominent economists are worried. In *Good Economics for Hard Times* (2019), the Nobel laureates Esther Duflo and Abhijit Banerjee call for a change of course and conclude:

> Economics is too important to be left to economists.

Or, as Robert Skidelsky puts it, in *What's Wrong with Economics* (2020):

> The task is no less than to reclaim economics for the humanities.

If Coleridge, Shelley, Scott and the others are looking down from Parnassus they would surely agree, and beg us to pay attention.

DANIEL DEFOE
1660-1731

Writing upon trade was the Whore I really doted upon,
and designed to have taken up with.

REVIEW, 1713

Daniel Defoe was some sixty years old when *Robinson Crusoe* appeared. He took to novel-writing after a long career as businessman, journalist, spy and poet. His *True Born Englishman* was, in its day, one of the best-selling poems ever published. He wrote it in reply to xenophobic attacks on King William III (a Dutchman). The poem portrays the British as the ultimate mongrel nation:

> In eager rapes, and furious lust begot,
> Betwixt a painted Britain and a Scot.
> Whose gend'ring offspring quickly learn'd to bow,
> And yoke their heifers to the Roman plough:
> From whence a mongrel half-bred race there came,
> With neither name, nor nation, speech nor fame
>
> *etc. etc.*

It was an age of absolute monarchies. In France

Louis XIV ruled by divine right, had powers of life and death, bled his country with pointless dynastic wars and organised the persecution of Protestants. Defoe fought all his life to spare England from such a fate. When James II showed signs of copying the Sun King, Defoe joined a rebellion. It failed and he was lucky to escape alive. He came to royal favour under William III and Mary Stuart, after the Glorious Revolution of 1688, but was soon back in trouble, when Queen Anne succeeded in 1702. The *Hymn to the Pillory* was a celebrated poetry 'happening'. Defoe was put in the pillory for a satirical attack on religious bigotry but he got his poem out first: it so pleased the crowd that he was treated as a hero and pelted, not with rubbish or stones, but with roses and garlands.

As a nonconformist in religion, Defoe could not attend Oxford or Cambridge. He began life as a merchant, traded in wool, hosiery and wine, ran a brickworks and dabbled in marine insurance. This last venture made him bankrupt, then a terrifying experience which marked him for life. He wrote about trade not as a journalist but from intimate knowledge of its risks and rewards. His heroes were not soldiers or saints but merchants, who stood for dissent, innovation – in a word, progress:

> Every new voyage the merchant contrives is a project; and ships are sent from port to port, as markets and merchandises differ, by the help of strange and universal intelligence—wherein some are so exquisite, so swift, and so exact, that a merchant

sitting at home in his counting-house at once con-
verses with all parts of the known world. This and
travel make a true-bred merchant the most intelli-
gent man in the world, and consequently the most
capable, when urged by necessity, to contrive new
ways to live.

This extract comes from Defoe's *Essay on Projects* of
1697, a rag-bag of proposals for the public benefit. Their
general thrust was to improve conditions for business.
Controversies about *laissez-faire* lay in the future. Defoe
was a pragmatist. His book was full of schemes for public
works. A national commission to improve the roads. A
commercial court, to settle trade disputes more quick-
ly. Shipping was especially risky, as Defoe well knew. He
proposed an insurance scheme for merchant sailors. Their
incentives should match the risks they faced, such as pi-
rate raids. Pay alone was not enough :

> For instance, a merchant ship coming home from
> the Indies, perhaps very rich, meets with a priva-
> teer … the captain calls up his crew, tells them,
> 'Gentlemen, you see how it is; I don't question but
> we may clear ourselves of this caper, if you will
> stand by me.' One of the crew, as willing to fight
> as the rest, and as far from a coward as the captain,
> but endowed with a little more wit than his fel-
> lows, replies, 'Noble captain, we are all willing to
> fight, and don't question but to beat him off; but

here is the case: if we are taken, we shall be set on shore and then sent home, and lose perhaps our clothes and a little pay; but if we fight and beat the privateer, perhaps half a score of us may be wounded and lose our limbs, and then we are undone and our families. If you will sign an obligation to us that the owners or merchants shall allow a pension to such as are maimed, that we may not fight for the ship, and go a-begging ourselves, we will bring off the ship or sink by her side; otherwise I am not willing to fight, for my part.' The captain cannot do this; so they strike, and the ship and cargo are lost.

Much as Defoe admired successful merchants, he expected them to pay their share in tax. A national commission should draw up a proper estimate of everyone's true worth, spare the poor and make sure that taxes fell on the broadest shoulders:

and he who was an overgrown rich tradesman of twenty or thirty thousand pounds estate should be taxed so, and plain English and plain dealing be practised indifferently throughout the kingdom; tradesmen and landed men should have neighbours' fare, as we call it, and a rich man should not be passed by when a poor man pays.

Defoe would be horrified that Robinson Crusoe's Caribbean island is now, most likely, a tax haven. He would see tax lawyers as pirates and want them strung up as such. He had a dire warning for tax dodgers:

> We read of the inhabitants of Constantinople, that they suffered their city to be lost for want of contributing in time for its defence, and pleaded poverty to their generous emperor when he went from house to house to persuade them; and yet when the Turks took it, the prodigious immense wealth they found in it, made them wonder at the sordid temper of the citizens.

Defoe's most far-sighted proposal concerned the Bank of England. It was founded in 1694, as a private concern with a public purpose: to raise money for the Crown. Defoe immediately saw its potential, both to strengthen the chaotic public finances and to support business activity across the nation. The reality fell far short. The bank was being run for the benefit of its owners, not the public – a view of banks that echoes down the ages:

> In short, it is only a great trade carried on for the private gain of a few concerned in the original stock; and though we are to hope for great things, because they have promised them, yet they are all future that we know of.
>
> And yet all this while a bank might be very beneficial to this kingdom; and this might be so, if either their own ingenuity or public authority

would oblige them to take the public good into equal concern with their private interest.

To explain what I mean: banks, being established by public authority, ought also, as all public things are, to be under limitations and restrictions from that authority; and those limitations being regulated with a proper regard to the ease of trade in general, and the improvement of the stock in particular, would make a bank a useful, profitable thing indeed.

Just three years after its foundation, Defoe proposed doubling the Bank of England's capital and extending its remit. The Bank should support trade and manufacturing up and down the Kingdom. If it would not come to the shires then the great and the good of each county should set up their own banks, to provide funds for local business:

These banks in their respective counties should be a general staple and factory for the manufactures of the said county, where every man that had goods made, might have money at a small interest for advance, the goods in the meantime being sent forward to market, to a warehouse for that purpose erected in London, where they should be disposed of to all the advantages the owner could expect, paying only 1 per cent. commission.

Defoe saw that people needed a home for their money.

They would lend to the Government, whatever their politics, as long as their money was safe. Banks were a good thing when properly run, as public utilities. Stock brokers and financial manipulators were another matter. Speculators undermined trust in the financial system which in turn harmed the real economy of goods and services. Speculation against the national credit should be illegal. He wanted to stamp it out, with taxes and regulations designed to:

> suppress this pernicious, growing Party … Then shall we Trade upon the square; Honesty and Industry will be the method of Thriving, and plain Trade be the General business of the Exchange.
>
> *Villainy of Stock Jobbers Detected,* 1701

Defoe renewed the attack on white collar crime with his *Anatomy of Exchange Alley* (1719). Stock jobbers were tantamount to traitors and worse than highwaymen, who at least spared widows and children and ran some personal risk:

> being sure to be hanged first or last, whereas [stock jobbers] rob only at the hazard of their Reputation which is generally lost before they begin.

His timing was perfect: the South Sea Bubble burst a year later. It was the greatest outbreak of financial mania in British history. When the crash came, many investors were ruined. Sir Isaac Newton lost a fortune, comment-

ing ruefully, 'I can calculate the movement of the stars
but not the madness of men.'

There were other prophetic words about credit in *The
Complete English Tradesman* (1722). Money is a social
construct and credit even more so, being entirely based
on trust. But credit has an almost magical transformative
power. Defoe, like others who came to economics from
the literary camp, seemed to have an intuitive feel for the
significance of money – as a sort of magnetic field operat-
ing on different laws to the real economy:

> Credit, next to real stock,* is the foundation, the
> life and soul, of business in a private tradesman; it
> is his prosperity; it is his support in the substance
> of his whole trade; even in public matters, it is the
> strength and fund of a nation …
>
> Credit makes war, and makes peace; raises
> armies, fits out navies, fights battles, besieges
> towns; and, in a word, it is more justly called the
> sinews of war than the money itself, because it can
> do all these things without money—nay, it will
> bring in money to be subservient, though it be in-
> dependent.
>
> Credit makes the soldier fight without pay, the
> armies march without provisions, and it makes
> tradesmen keep open shop without stock. The

---

* Throughout these extracts, 'stock' means 'capital', ie the tradesman's
own funds or 'equity' in the business.

force of credit is not to be described by words; it is an impregnable fortification, either for a nation, or for a single man in business; and he that has credit is invulnerable, whether he has money or no; nay, it will make money … it makes paper pass for money, and fills the Exchequer and the banks with as many millions as it pleases, upon demand.

A thriving economy needed a strong flow of credit. And credit rested on confidence, which had to be earned and managed with the utmost care:

As credit is a coy mistress, and will not easily be courted, so she is a mighty nice touchy lady, and is soon affronted; if she is ill used, she flies at once and it is a very doubtful thing whether ever you gain her favour again …

Kings, princes, emperors, it is all one: nay, a private shopkeeper shall borrow money much easier than a prince, if the credit of the tradesman has the reputation of being an honest man. Not the crown itself can give credit to the head that wears it, if once he that wears it comes but to mortgage his honour in the matter of payment of money.

The *Complete English Tradesman* is a manual for the aspiring merchant. It was the fruit of bitter experience. Defoe had made most of the mistakes he warned his readers against and had lost his wife's fortune in the process.

The book covers every aspect of a merchant's life – how to run his shop, his accounts, his marriage, his correspondence and above all his customers, who are to be his idols. A shopkeeper must put up with every whim:

> A tradesman behind his counter must have no flesh and blood about him, no passion, no resentment … What impertinences, what taunts, flouts and ridiculous things he must bear in his business, and must not show the least return … if his real temper be fiery and hot, he must show none of it in his shop – he must be a perfect complete hypocrite if he will be a complete tradesman.

Retail therapy was already a feature of life in the 1720s. Defoe imagines a lady customer demanding to inspect bolt after bolt of cloth, spending nothing and leaving without a word:

> —Did your Ladyship try him as you said you would?
> —Try him! I believe he has tumbled three thousand pounds' worth of goods for me.

Having endured all this with imperturbable calm ('*Madam, I shall be very glad if I can be so happy as to please you … don't speak of trouble for that is the duty of our trade …* '), the merchant goes on to sell her goods worth £60 and acquires a customer for life. There is a whole chapter on the *Customary Frauds of Trade,* among which

Defoe lists sales patter, advertising and shop design. The customer expects a degree of licence but things can go too far:

> The shopkeeper ought indeed to have a good tongue. But he should not make a common prostitute of his tongue … there is a modest liberty, which trading licence, like the poetic licence, allows to all tradesmen of every kind: but tradesmen ought no more to lie behind the counter than parsons ought to talk treason in the pulpit.

Above all, the book conveys the sheer pleasure of the game, for all its many dangers:

> Now in order to have a man apply heartily, and pursue earnestly, the business he is engaged in, there is yet another thing necessary, namely that he should delight in it.

The *Tour through the Whole Island of Great Britain* is a pæan to Britain's booming commerce. Defoe was, on the whole, sympathetic to the poor. But there were blind spots such as child labour, which he tends to celebrate as a sign of a thriving community. In Taunton, for instance:

> One of the chief manufacturers of the town told us that there was at that time so good a trade in the town, that they had eleven hundred looms going for the weaving of sagathies, du roys, and

such kind of stuffs and … not one of those looms
wanted work. He further added, that there was not
a child in the town, or in the villages round it, of
above five years old, but, if it was not neglected by
its parents and untaught, could earn its own bread.

Later on the *Tour* he watches a recruiting sergeant at
work in a manufacturing town. A merchant standing by
him observes that

not a poor child above four years old but could
get its own bread, besides there being so good a
trade at this time, causes us to advance wages a lit-
tle… and while it is so they may beat the heads out
of their drums, if they will, they'll get no soldiers
here; but let them come when trade is dead, and
the people want work, and they may get soldiers
enough.

In a word, adds Defoe, *'tis poverty and starving that
fills armies, not trade and manufacturing.* There is a mov-
ing account in the *Tour* of coming upon a miner's wife
in the Derbyshire peaks. She lives in a cave with her hus-
band and five children. He works in a lead mine and she
helps wash the ore. Between them they can earn eight
pennies in a good day. They find her husband emerging
from his pit:

he was as lean as a skeleton, pale as a dead corpse
… his flesh lank, and, as we thought, something of

the colour of the lead itself … beside his basket of
tools, he brought up with him about three quar-
ters of a hundred weight of ore.

The miner talks a dialect so strange that they need an
interpreter. Through him they learn that the miner works
sixty fathoms deep and wishes he could go deeper, to find
a richer seam. There is a long description of the cave, the
pit and the life led within them:

> If we blessed ourselves before, when we saw how
> the poor woman and her five children lived in the
> hole or cave in the mountain … we had much more
> room to reflect how much we had to acknowledge
> to our maker, that we were not appointed to get
> our bread thus, one hundred and fifty yards under
> ground, or in a hole as deep in the earth as the
> cross upon St Paul's cupola is high out of it. Nor
> was it possible to see these miserable people with-
> out such reflections, unless you will suppose a man
> as stupid and senseless as the horse he rides on.

There were moments of pessimism about the econo-
my. Could the market outgrow itself and go into decline
for lack of demand?

> There may be as many Goods made in England
> as ever, but if there are not as many sold as ever,
> the Trade will be allowed to decline; nay, the
> more there is made, the more the Manufacture is

declined if they cannot be sold, because the Quantity becomes a Grievance to itself.

At heart, though, Defoe was an optimist. The system would deliver, if allowed to. Abundant credit, buoyant wages and investment would spark a virtuous circle. All classes could and should benefit. Decent wages would improve productivity and boost spending power :

> As the people get greater wages, so they, I mean the same poorer part of the people, clothe better, and furnish better, and this increases the consumption of the very manufactures they make; then that consumption increases the quantity made, and this creates what we call inland trade, by which innumerable families are employed, and the increase of the people maintained, and by which increase of trade and people the present growing prosperity of this nation is produced.
>
> *Complete English Trader*

Here speaks one of the great stirrers of those 'animal spirits' which, according to Keynes, are the real motor of economic growth.* Defoe could tell a stock from a flow.

---

* 'Enterprise only pretends to itself to be mainly actuated by the statements in its own prospectus… Only a little more than an expedition to the South Pole, is it based on an exact calculation of benefits to come. Thus if the animal spirits are dimmed, and the spontaneous optimism falters, leaving us to depend on nothing but a mathematical expectation, enterprise will fade and die.' *General Theory*

The world of the gentry might stagnate but not that of the merchant. As he never tired of saying, *An estate's a pond but a trade's a spring*. The power of self-interest, coupled with the sheer pleasure of a good venture, would keep things turning:

> Men in Trade, more especially than the rest of mankind, are bound by their interest; gain is the end of commerce, where that gain visibly attends the adventurer, as no hazard can discourage, so no other obligation can prevent the application.'
>
> *Essay on Loans,* 1710

Robinson Crusoe is on a slaving expedition when his ship is driven onto the rocks (if he is being punished by God, as he fears, it is not for being a slave-trader but for ignoring his father's advice and running off to sea). In the first half of the book Crusoe gradually provides himself with a plot of corn, a flock of goats, a supply of dried raisins, and safe place of shelter. He learns to bake bread which leads him to reflect on the division of labour:

> 'tis a little wonderful, and what I believe few people have thought much upon, *viz*. the strange multitude of little things necessary in the providing, producing, curing, dressing, making and finishing this one article of bread.

In his first days on the island, before the stricken ship finally disappears, Crusoe has a chance to rescue a few stores. As he ponders what to take, he sees that gold is worthless:

> I smiled to myself at the sight of this money. 'O Drug!' said I aloud, 'what art thou good for? Thou art not worth to me, no, not the taking off of the ground: one of those knives is worth all this heap; I have no manner of use for thee, e'en remain where thou art and go to the bottom, as a creature whose life is not worth saving.' However, upon second thoughts I took it away; and wrapping all this in a piece of canvas, I began to think of making another raft.

According to mercantilism (the reigning belief of the day), gold was the source of wealth and the aim of economic policy was to amass as much of it as possible by running a trade surplus. The 'O Drug' speech seems to overturn a creed which Defoe himself accepted. Coleridge compared it to Shakespeare. It is the endless scope for reading ideas into *Robinson Crusoe* that makes it such a universal book; perhaps why it has left such a footprint on the literature of economics. Four years on, Crusoe has all he needs to survive. He sees that his real needs are few and avarice is absurd:

> But all I could make use of was all that was valuable. I had enough to eat and supply my wants, and what was all the rest to me? If I killed more flesh than I could eat, the dog must eat it, or the vermin

… the nature and experience of things dictated to me, upon just reflection, that all the good things of this world are of no farther good to us, than they are for our use …

The most covetous, griping miser in the world would have been cured of the vice … if he had been in my case; for I possessed infinitely more than I knew what to do with. I had, as I hinted before, a parcel of money, as well as gold and silver, about thirty six pounds sterling. Alas! there the nasty sorry useless stuff lay: I had no manner of business for it … I would have given it all for sixpenny worth of turnip and carrot seed.

One might ask what a solitary man on a desert island has to do with the study of money, markets and exchange. But economics builds its vast edifice on the atomised individual, striving to 'maximise his utility'. Crusoe was the ideal laboratory specimen. Marx used him in *Das Kapital* to explain his labour theory of value, by depicting a primitive economy where the necessities of life have not yet become 'commodities'. Others followed and before long no self-respecting work on economics was without its Crusoe parable. All this would have mystified Defoe. His economic message is simple: an economy is naturally buoyant. Trade will thrive where it is free to do so, especially when oiled with a good supply of credit. It is:

an unexhausted current, which not only fills the
pond and keeps it full, but is continually running
over, and fills all the lower ponds and places about
it.

Or, as Adam Smith later put it:

Little else is requisite to carry a state to the highest
degree of opulence from the lowest barbarism, but
peace, easy taxes, and a tolerable administration
of justice; all the rest being brought about by the
natural course of things.

The nature of this opulence, its distribution and social con-
sequences would be for a later age to worry over.

JONATHAN SWIFT
1667-1745

Towards the end of his travels, Gulliver arrives in the land of the Houyhnhnms. These philosophical horses rule over a race of humanoid brutes called Yahoos. Gulliver has a Houyhnhnm master who treats him kindly, as a Yahoo with some sparks of intelligence. Gulliver tells his master about life among the 'Yahoos' back in Britain:

> I was at much pains to describe to him the use of money, the materials it was made of, and the value of the metals; that when a Yahoo had got a great store of this precious substance, he was able to purchase whatever he had a mind to; the finest clothing, the noblest houses, great tracts of land, the most costly meats and drinks, and have his choice of the most beautiful females. Therefore since money alone was able to perform all these feats, our Yahoos thought they could never have enough of it to spend, or to save, as they found

themselves inclined, from their natural bent either
to profusion or avarice; that the rich man enjoyed
the fruit of the poor man's labour, and the latter
were a thousand to one in proportion to the
former; that the bulk of our people were forced
to live miserably, by labouring every day for small
wages, to make a few live plentifully.

I enlarged myself much on these, and many
other particulars to the same purpose; but his
honour was still to seek; for he went upon a
supposition, that all animals had a title to their
share in the productions of the earth.

A few pages later the Houyhnhnm observes that he has
seen the same lust for gold among the Yahoos of his own
country. He now begins to understand it better and tells
Gulliver that:

in some fields of his country there are certain
shining stones of several colours, whereof the
Yahoos are violently fond: and when part of these
stones is fixed in the earth, as it sometimes happens,
they will dig with their claws for whole days to get
them out; then carry them away, and hide them by
heaps in their kennels; but still looking round with
great caution, for fear their comrades should find
out their treasure. My master said he could never
discover the reason of this unnatural appetite, or
how these stones could be of any use to a Yahoo;

but now he believed it might proceed from the same principle of avarice which I had ascribed to mankind.

Jonathan Swift, the author of *Gulliver's Travels*, was a journalist, a poet, a political pundit and a priest. On the evidence of these extracts he was no believer in 'rational economic man'. Nor was he much taken with economic progress. Like most priests in those days Swift supported the traditional order, a society governed by the landowning class and the established Church. He saw bankers and 'stock jobbers' as a disruptive force, with too much power and a tendency to religious dissent. He wrote a few articles for the London papers giving vent to these views but only paid serious attention to the economy after moving back to Ireland (in 1714), as Dean of St Patrick's Cathedral, Dublin.

Swift was raised in Ireland, the son of an English family. As Dean of the Protestant cathedral he belonged to the ruling class. However, he was appalled by the state of the country and soon fell out with the government. Under laws imposed from London, the Irish had to send their wool to England for processing. They were forbidden to export finished cloth and had to use English ships for all their overseas trade. Huge tracts of land belonged to absentee landlords, who lived in England on the back of a half-starved Irish peasantry. The country was sunk in misery. Swift went on the attack in 1720, with *A Proposal for the Universal Use of Irish Manufacture*:

The fable in Ovid of Arachne and Pallas, is to this purpose. The goddess had heard of one Arachne a young virgin, very famous for spinning and weaving. They both met upon a trial of skill; and Pallas finding herself almost equalled in her own art, stung with rage and envy, knocked her rival down, turned her into a spider, enjoining her to spin and weave for ever, out of her own bowels, and in a very narrow compass. I confess, that from a boy I always pitied poor Arachne, and could never heartily love the goddess on account of so cruel and unjust a sentence; which however is fully executed upon us by England, with further additions of rigour and severity. For the greatest part of our bowels and vitals are extracted, without allowing us the liberty of spinning and weaving them.

As the Irish were not allowed to sell their goods to others they could at least sell to themselves. Why not ban the wearing of

any cloth or stuff in their families, which were not of the growth and manufacture of this kingdom? What if they had extended it so far as utterly to exclude all silks, velvets, calicoes, and the whole lexicon of female fopperies; and declared, that whoever acted otherwise, should be deemed and reputed an enemy to the nation? … What if the ladies would be content with Irish stuffs for the furniture of their houses, for gowns and petticoats to themselves and their daughters? Upon the whole, and to crown all the rest: Let a firm resolution be taken by male and female, never to appear with one single shred that comes from England.

The pamphlet hit a nerve. Its printer was prosecuted. Swift took his revenge with a stream of lampoons on all involved in the trial (which was eventually dropped). In 1726 he obtained a private meeting in London with the Prime Minister, hoping to obtain a change of policy. As Walpole paid no notice, Swift returned to the charge with *The Present Miserable State of Ireland* (1727). English cloth weavers had prevailed on Parliament to impose unjust restrictions on their Irish competitors. The end result was a political and economic disaster for both countries:

An act (as the event plainly shows) fuller of greediness than good policy; an act as beneficial to France and Spain, as it has been destructive to England and Ireland. At the passing of this fatal act, the condition of our trade was glorious and flourishing, though no way interfering with the English … slight half-works, and gaudy stuffs, were the only product of our looms: these were partly consumed by the meanest of our people, and partly sent to the northern nations, from which we had in exchange, timber, iron, hemp, flax, pitch, tar, and hard dollars. At the time the current money of Ireland was foreign silver, a man could hardly receive 100 pounds, without finding the coin of all the northern powers, and every prince of the empire among it. This money was returned into England for fine cloths, silks, &c. for our own wear, for rents, for coals, for hardware, and all other English manufactures, and, in a great measure, supplied the London merchants with foreign silver for exportation.

The repeated clamours of the English weavers produced this act, so destructive to themselves and us. They looked with envious eyes upon our prosperity, and complained of being undersold by us in those commodities, which they themselves did not deal in. At their instances the act was passed, and we lost our profitable northern trade. Have they got it? No, surely, you have found they have ever since declined in the trade they so happily possessed.

It was a classic example of a trade war that leaves all sides worse off. Swift followed up with *A Short View of the State of Ireland* (1728), arguing that Ireland had the skills and resources to earn its way, if London would only allow it:

Ireland is the only kingdom I ever heard or read of, either in ancient or modern story, which was denied the liberty of exporting their native commodities and manufactures wherever they pleased …

I should be glad to know, by what secret method it is, that we grow a rich and flourishing people, without liberty, trade, manufactures, inhabitants, money, or the privilege of coining; without industry, labour or improvement of land; and with more than half the rent and profits of the whole kingdom annually exported, for which we receive not a single farthing.

Most English readers at the time would have viewed Ireland with a mixture of condescension and anti-Catholic prejudice. They needed a jolt. With his *Modest Proposal* of 1729, Swift produced an armour-piercing satire. Having solemnly computed that 120,000 surplus children were born each year in Ireland and shown that rearing them made no economic sense, Swift comes to his 'modest proposal':

I have been assured by a very knowing American of my acquaintance in London, that a young healthy child well nursed, is, at a year old, a most delicious nourishing and wholesome food, whether stewed, roasted, baked, or boiled …

I do therefore humbly offer it to publick consideration, that of the hundred and twenty thousand children, already computed, twenty thousand may be reserved for breed, whereof only one fourth part to be males; which is more than we allow to sheep, black cattle, or swine, and my reason is, that these children are seldom the fruits of marriage, a circumstance not much regarded by our savages, therefore, one male will be sufficient to serve four females. That the remaining hundred thousand may, at a year old, be offered in sale to the persons of quality and fortune, through the kingdom, always advising the mother to let them suck plentifully in the last month, so as to render them plump, and fat for a good table …

I have already computed the charge of nursing a beggar's child (in which list I reckon all cottagers, labourers, and four-fifths of the farmers) to be about two shillings per annum, rags included; and I believe no gentleman would repine to give ten shillings for the carcass of a good fat child, which, as I have said, will make four dishes of excellent nutritive meat, when he hath only some particular friend, or his own family to dine with him. Thus the squire will learn to be a good landlord, and grow popular among his tenants, the mother will have eight shillings neat profit, and be fit for work till she produces another child.

Those who are more thrifty (as I must confess the times require) may flay the carcass; the skin of which, artificially dressed, will make admirable gloves for ladies, and summer boots for fine gentlemen.

As for the existing adult population:

> Some persons of a desponding spirit are in great concern about that vast number of poor people, who are aged, diseased, or maimed; and I have been desired to employ my thoughts what course may be taken, to ease the nation of so grievous an incumbrance. But I am not in the least pain upon that matter, because it is very well known, that they are every day dying, and rotting, by cold and famine, and filth, and vermin, as fast as can be reasonably expected.

All the advantages of eating Irish babies are solemnly rehearsed, all the objections carefully dismissed (the pamphlet was also a lampoon of 'Projectors', such as Defoe, who abounded at the time). Finally there a glimpse of the alternatives, such as a tax on absentee landlords, or 'buying Irish':

> Therefore let no man talk to me of other expedients: Of taxing our absentees at five shillings a pound: Of using neither clothes, nor household furniture, except what is of our own growth and manufacture.

A nation that cannot mint its own currency is always

at a disadvantage. This was Ireland's case. Swift complained repeatedly about the *extra burden of exchange* caused by the widespread use of foreign coinage in Ireland. Sharp-witted bankers could exploit these differences in value. In *A Short View*, Swift had already railed against:

> Those worthy gentlemen the BANKERS; who … are the only thriving people among us: and I have often wished, that a law were enacted to hang up half a dozen bankers every year, and thereby interpose, at least some short delay to the farther ruin of Ireland.

Any measure from London affecting the currency was bound to be controversial. In 1724 the government granted a patent to an English metal dealer, William Wood, to mint halfpenny coins for Ireland. At the time, even copper coins were meant to be worth their face value when melted down for metal. It was widely believed that Wood's coins would be of base metal; that it was a licence to exchange scrap metal for silver; and that he had bribed the King's mistress to obtain the patent. Whether or not the coins were bad, London had no right to impose them without consultation. Swift wrote a series of protests under the assumed name of M. B. Drapier, a Dublin tradesman. Their general thrust was that the coins were worthless, that only the King's coin was legal tender, and consequently that the Irish need not, and must not, accept Wood's halfpennies:

At last one Mr Wood, a mean ordinary man, a hardware-dealer, procured a patent under his majesty's broad seal to coin £108,000, in copper for this kingdom … Now you must know, that the halfpence and farthings in England pass for very little more than they are worth; and if you should beat them to pieces, and sell them to the brasier, you would not lose much above a penny in a shilling. Bur Mr. Wood made his halfpence of such base metal, and so much smaller than the English ones, that the brasier would hardly give you above a penny of good money for a shilling* of his; so that this sum of 108,000 *l.* in good gold and silver, must be given for trash, that will not be worth above eight or nine thousand pounds real value.

Gresham's Law, one of the oldest in economics, says that bad money will drive out good. When the Government debases the coinage, people hold onto their good coins and spend with the debased ones, if they can. Wood's corrupt coinage would drain gold and silver from the Irish economy and by reducing the flow of money, leave everyone worse off:

But you may take my word, whenever this money gains footing among you, you will be utterly undone … Do you think I will sell you a yard of

* There were 12 pennies (*d.*) in a shilling (*s.*) and 20 shillings in a pound (*l.*)

tenpenny stuff for twenty of Mr. Wood's halfpence? No, not under two hundred at least; neither will I be at the trouble of counting, but weigh them in a lump. I will tell you one thing farther, that if Mr. Wood's project should take, it would ruin even our beggars; for when I give a beggar a halfpenny, it will quench his thirst, or go a good way to fill his belly; but the twelfth part of a halfpenny will do him no more service than if I should give him three pins out of my sleeve.

There were seven Drapier's letters, covering the various legal moves and counter-moves, as well as ballads and satires designed for the crowd. He even used the pulpit – this is from Swift's sermon *On Doing Good*:

Perhaps it may be thought by some, that this way of discoursing is not so proper from the pulpit. But surely, when an open attempt is made, and far carried on, to make a great kingdom one large poorhouse, to deprive us of all means to exercise hospitality or charity, to turn our cities and churches into ruins, to make the country a desert for wild beasts and robbers, to destroy all arts and sciences, all trades and manufactures, and the very tillage of the ground, only to enrich one obscure ill-designing projector, and his followers; it is time for the pastor to cry out that the wolf is getting into his flock.

Swift's first three letters focussed on Wood and the coins. By the fourth letter, emboldened by massive popular support, he was telling the Irish:

> by the laws of GOD, of NATURE, of NATIONS, and of your COUNTRY, you ARE and OUGHT to be as FREE a people as your brethren in England.

This was brave. It was one thing to attack Wood. To attack, even by implication, the colonial regime in Ireland was quite another. Swift's printer, John Harding, was arrested and a reward of £300 offered for proof of the Drapier's identity. Sir Walter Scott, in his *Life* of Swift, describes how he went immediately to plead with the Lord Lieutenant (effectively the Governor of Ireland):

> Swift, bold in the merit of his cause, and in the support of the people, was not to be appalled by this menacing procedure: he went to the levee of the Lord Lieutenant, burst through the circle with which he was surrounded, and, in a firm and stern voice, demanded of Lord Carteret the meaning of these severities against a poor industrious tradesman, who had published two or three papers designed for the good of the country. Carteret, to whom Swift was personally well known, and who could have no doubt of his being the author of the Drapier's letters, evaded the expostulation by an apt and elegant quotation from Virgil:

> Res dura, et regni novitas, me talia cogunt
> Moliri.*

The courtly circle, astounded at the daring conduct of Swift, were delighted and reassured by the Lord Lieutenant's presence of mind and urbanity.

Scott's account continues:

> while Harding was in jail, Swift actually visited him in the disguise of an Irish country clown or *spalpeen*. Some of the printer's family or friends, who chanced to visit him at the same time, were urging him to earn his own release, by informing against the author of the Drapier's Letters. Harding replied steadily, that he would rather perish in jail before he would be guilty of such treachery and baseness. All this passed in Swift's presence, who sat beside them in silence, and heard, with apparent indifference, a discussion which might be said to involve his ruin. He came and departed without being known to anyone but Harding.

Whether or not this second anecdote is true, it is of a piece with Swift's efforts to free Harding. One of the

---

* The extract from Virgil (spoken by Queen Dido) means: *Hard necessity and the newness of my reign oblige me to such measures…*

Such was the language of public life in the 1720s! Walter Scott began his literary career by editing the works of Swift. He later wrote a series of pamphlets in defence of the Scottish pound note, much on the lines of the Drapier's Letters – see the chapter on Scott.

Drapier's letters is an address to the Grand Jury who were to try Harding. It concludes with a poem:

> Assist your patriot in your own defence.
> That stupid cant, he went too far, despise,
> And know, that to be brave is to be wise:
> Think how he struggled for your liberty,
> And give him freedom while yourselves are free.

The crowd loved it. Wood's patent could not be enforced and was quietly dropped. Swift became a national hero.*

This next passage, from a subsequent pamphlet, has put Swift among the prophets of the Laffer curve – the idea that higher tax rates can lead to lower revenues:

> But I will tell you a secret, which I learned many years ago from the commissioners of the customs in London; they said, when any commodity appeared to be taxed above a moderate rate, the consequence was, to lessen that branch of the revenue by one half; ... in the business of laying impositions, two and two never made more than one; which happens by lessening the import, and the strong temptation of running [i.e. smuggling] such goods as paid high duties.

---

* But Harding died in prison, too soon to benefit from the Government's climb down. David Nokes, (*Jonathan Swift, a Hypocrite Reversed*, OUP 1985) concludes: 'It was the forgotten printer, John Harding, not the celebrated Dean, Jonathan Swift, who was the real martyr of the campaign against Wood.'

The Laffer curve fed into Reaganomics and the low-tax supply-side revolution of the 1980s. Swift's support for this agenda must be moot, given his general distaste for bankers, absentee landlords and the like. But he was certainly no supporter of handouts. People should earn their own living. This was both a duty and – except for the poor Irish – a right. He did however make a lasting contribution to 'supply-side reform' with his loan fund, designed to help *industrious tradesmen* make a start in business. Swift put £500 into the fund, then a substantial sum. The loans were small – £5 or £10 at a time; were repaid in weekly instalments of a few shillings; and carried no interest. Borrowers had to obtain two guarantors. Swift insisted on being repaid and stood ready to sue. The scheme must have worked: over time, similar funds spread across Ireland and beyond. Swift is often credited as one of the fathers of the modern micro-credit movement, which now helps poor families in many parts of the world as they take their first steps towards financial independence.

We have come to see markets as disembodied, random and rather ominous forces – the labour market, the oil market, the stock market. These sorts of 'markets' have stolen the name from proper markets, where small traders stand behind their stalls and banter with the public. The produce is often local, presented with knowledge and pride. For much of history and still in much of the world, this is the meaning of a 'market': a place to stock up for the week and meet people, or, for the traders, to scrape a modest living. Swift captured the human side of market life in this poignant little poem on *Market Women's Cries*:

APPLES

Come buy my fine wares,
Plums, apples and pears.
A hundred a penny,
In conscience too many:
Come, will you have any?
My children are seven,
I wish them in Heaven;
My husband's a sot,
With his pipe and his pot,
Not a farthen will gain them,
And I must maintain them.

ONIONS

Come, follow me by the smell,
Here are delicate onions to sell;
I promise to use you well.
They make the blood warmer,
You'll feed like a farmer;
For this is every cook's opinion,
No savoury dish without an onion;
But, lest your kissing should be spoiled,
Your onions must be thoroughly boiled:

> Or else you may spare
> Your mistress a share,
> The secret will never be known:
> She cannot discover
> The breath of her lover,
> But think it as sweet as her own.

HERRINGS

> Be not sparing,
> Leave off swearing.
> Buy my herring
> Fresh from Malahide,
> Better never was tried.
> Come, eat them with pure fresh butter and mustard,
> Their bellies are soft, and as white as a custard.
> Come, sixpence a dozen, to get me some bread,
> Or, like my own herrings, I soon shall be dead.

Swift asked no favours for Ireland, just the right to earn a living. The Irish economy went on declining. It took the Great Famine of the 1840s to remind the Government of its laissez-faire instincts. Precious little was done for the victims. Over a million died of hunger, though exports of Irish food continued apace. The cold fury of *A Modest Proposal* seemed more than ever justified. Swift's epitaph – which he wrote himself – is near his tomb in St Patrick's Cathedral, 'where savage indignation can no longer tear his heart'.

PERCY BYSSHE SHELLEY
1792-1822

Hence commerce springs, the venal interchange
Of all that human art or Nature yield;
Which wealth should purchase not, but want demand,
And natural kindness hasten to supply
From the full fountain of its boundless love.

QUEEN MAB

Percy Bysshe Shelley came of age towards the end of the Napoleonic wars. He was heir to a baronetcy and a large estate in Sussex. He was also a penniless poet with radical views that marked him as a danger to polite society. Wartime Britain was a dangerous place for dissidents. Shelley supported the ideals of the French revolution. He thought the threat to ordinary working people came less from France than from the ruling British elite.

In principle Shelley had no time for political economy. A poet's business was with higher matters:

> Ethical science arranges the elements which poetry
> has created, and propounds schemes and proposes
> examples of civil and domestic life: nor is it for
> want of admirable doctrines that men hate, and

despise, and censure, and deceive, and subjugate one another. But poetry acts in another and diviner manner.

A Defence of Poetry, 1821

But life for the masses was dreadful. Shelley yearned to do something. He began to engage with the dismal science. Adam Smith's *Wealth of Nations* appeared in 1776. The 'invisible hand' – the idea that self-interest can serve the general good – was never likely to appeal to Shelley. But there was much else in the book to interest him. Adam Smith overturned the mercantilist view that gold was the source of wealth. Consumption was *the sole end and purpose of all production.* The true source of value was labour, hence hoarding gold was pointless. Moreover, Smith much disliked unearned incomes such as landed rent. Luxury and display by the idle rich reduced the pool of capital for productive investment. Shelley's *Queen Mab* (1813) is the work of a young and passionate poet: it would probably not have impressed Adam Smith but it clearly drew on his work. It is an assault on religion, tyranny, commerce and the subversion of free love, dressed up as a visit to the Fairy Queen, from whose castle in the sky we look down on human life through the ages. There are prose notes, including an extensive one to these lines:

And statesmen boast
Of wealth!

In it Shelley tackles the true nature of wealth:

There is no real wealth but the labour of man. Were the mountains of gold and the valleys of silver, the world would not be one grain of corn the richer; no one comfort would be added to the human race. In consequence of our consideration for the precious metals, one man is enabled to heap to himself luxuries at the expense of the necessaries of his neighbour; a system admirably fitted to produce all the varieties of disease and crime, which never fail to characterise the two extremes of opulence and penury…

The poor are set to labour, – for what? Not the food for which they famish: not the blankets for want of which their babes are frozen by the cold of their miserable hovels: not those comforts of civilisation without which civilised man is far more miserable than the meanest savage … no; for the pride of power, for the miserable isolation of pride, for the false pleasures of the hundredth part of society…

English reformers exclaim against sinecures, – but the true pension list is the rent-roll of the landed proprietors: wealth a power usurped by the few, to compel the many to labour for their benefit. The laws which support this system derive their force from the ignorance and credulity of its victims: they are the result of a conspiracy of the few against the many.

Shelley added a plea for a shorter working day. The idea came from his father-in-law, the utilitarian philosopher Godwin:

> The commodities that substantially contribute to the subsistence of the human species form a very short catalogue: they demand from us but a slender portion of industry. If these only were produced, and sufficiently produced, the species of man would be continued. If the labour necessarily required to produce them were equitably divided among the poor, and, still more, if it were equitably divided among all, each man's share of labour would be light, and his portion of leisure would be ample …
>
> It is a calculation of [Godwin], that all the conveniences of civilised life might be produced, if society would divide the labour equally among its members, by each individual being employed in labour two hours during the day.

Shelley printed a few copies of *Queen Mab* for private circulation. Such a subversive poem could not be published in a Britain still at war. It eventually became a radical's bible, but only after Shelley's death.

His next pamphlet met a similar fate. In 1817 Princess Charlotte died in childbirth. She was much mourned. Around the same time, three labourers were hanged and then beheaded for leading the Pentridge Rising. A government spy had egged them on; their trial was summary and their execution smacked of judicial murder. In his *Address to the People on the Death of Princess Charlotte* Shelley set these deaths side by side and urged his readers to mourn for their freedoms, not for the princess. There was now a new threat to freedom: the national debt. The Government had borrowed around £900m – nearer £90bn in today's money – to pay for the Napoleonic wars. It was the poor who paid the interest on this debt – some £45m p.a. – and wealthy bond-holders who received it, as unearned income. The market in war bonds was controlled by 'stock jobbers', speculators in search of a quick profit:

> The effect of this debt is to produce such an unequal distribution of the means of living as saps the foundation of social union and civilised life. It creates a double aristocracy, instead of one which was sufficiently burdensome before, and gives twice as many people the liberty of living in luxury and idleness on the produce of the industrious and the poor …
>
> They are not like the old aristocracy, men of pride and honour *sans peur et sans tache*,* but petty piddling slaves who have gained a right to the title of public creditors, either by gambling in the funds,† or by subserviency to Government, or by some other villainous trade …

* 'Sans peur et sans tache' = fearless men of honour unstained.
† Funds = government bonds.

The effect of this system is that the day-labourer gains no more now by working sixteen hours a day than he gained before by working eight. I put the thing in its simplest and most intelligible shape. The labourer, he that tills the ground, and manufactures cloth, is the man who has to provide out of what he would bring home to his wife and children for the luxuries and comforts of those whose claims are represented by an annuity of forty-four millions a year levied upon the English nation.

Shelley's view of the national debt must have been coloured by his opposition to the war, and perhaps by his dealings with moneylenders (before coming into a regular allowance, he lived mainly off money borrowed against his inheritance). But he had a serious point: that the wealthy had used their control of Parliament to abolish income tax and offload the bill for the war onto the backs of the labouring poor. When the poor demanded a proper voice in Parliament – no taxation without representation – the authorities had responded with violence and judicial murder.

After the war ended in 1815 a general slump deepened the misery. No protest was tolerated. The excesses of the French revolution were still a vivid memory. In 1819 a peaceful demonstration at Peterloo turned into a massacre. A squadron of cavalry charged into the crowd leaving eighteen dead and six hundred wounded, among them women and children. Shelley was by now living in Italy.* He dashed off *The Mask of Anarchy* in protest. It begins with the famous image of Castlereagh, a member of the Government widely blamed for the repression:

> I met Murder on the way -
> He had a mask like Castlereagh -
> Very smooth he looked, yet grim;
> Seven bloodhounds followed him:

It ends, some ninety verses later, with the great chorus:

> Rise like lions after slumber
> In unvanquishable number —
> Shake your chains to earth like dew
> Which in sleep had fallen on you
> Ye are many – they are few.

On the way, it opens a new line of attack on the whole financial system (The italics are mine). What, he asks, is slavery to the poor?

> 'Tis to see your children weak
> With their mothers pine and peak,
> When the winter winds are bleak,–
> They are dying whilst I speak.

---

* 'Byron, who was living nearby, had used his maiden speech in the House of Lords (in 1812) to plead for leniency towards the 'Nottingham frame-breakers'. These were the original Luddites, who set out to destroy the machines which had ruined their livelihood.

'Tis to hunger for such diet
As the rich man in his riot
Casts to the fat dogs that lie
Surfeiting beneath his eye;

'Tis to let the Ghost of Gold
Take from Toil a thousandfold
More than e'er its substance could
In the tyrannies of old.

Paper coin – that forgery
Of the title-deeds, which ye
Hold to something of the worth
Of the inheritance of Earth.

The poem was explosive. Shelley's publisher in London, would be the one to face prosecution. Understandably, he sat on it (the poem finally appeared in 1832). Meanwhile Shelley set about a much fuller statement, the *Philosophical View of Reform*. He first showed how the country was controlled by a wealthy few:

> The power which has increased therefore is the power of the rich. The name and office of king is merely the mask of this power and is a kind of stalking horse used to conceal these 'catchers of men' while they lay their nets. Monarchy is only the string which ties the robber's bundle.

Not content with political control, the ruling oligarchy had vastly reinforced their power through *the device of public credit*. By this Shelley meant the whole system of credit, banking and the national debt which had emerged since Defoe's day:

> Now this device is one of those execrable contrivances of misrule which overbalance the materials of common advantage produced by the progress of civilisation and increase the number of those who are idle in proportion to those who work, whilst it increases, through the factitious wants of those indolent, privileged persons, the quantity of work to be done. The rich, no longer being able to rule by force, have invented this scheme that they may rule by fraud.

Governments in every age had debased the currency, by mixing gold with lesser metals. But now bankers could summon credit out of thin air and lend it to the ruling class. It was a tool for oppressing the poor by eating into their purchasing power:

> But the modern scheme of public credit is a far subtler and more complicated contrivance of misrule. All great transactions of personal property in England are managed by signs and that is by the authority of the possessor expressed upon paper, thus representing in a compendious form his right to so much gold, which represents his right to so much labour. A man may write on a piece of paper what he pleases; he may say he is worth a thousand

when he is not worth a hundred pounds. If he can make others believe this, he has credit for the sum to which his name is attached. And so long as this credit lasts, he can enjoy all the advantages which would arise out of the actual possession of that sum he is believed to possess. He can lend two hundred to this man and three to that other, and his bills, among those who believe that he possesses this sum, pass like money.

Of course in the same proportion as bills of this sort, beyond the actual goods or gold and silver possessed by the drawer, pass current, they defraud those who have gold and silver and goods of the advantages legally attached to the possession of them, and they defraud the labourer and artisan ... whilst they render wages fluctuating and add to the toil of the cultivator and manufacturer.

Shelley is saying that credit creates purchasing power. The banks could lend money well beyond the gold they had on deposit. This 'extra' money – which gave one man command over another man's labour – was summoned out of thin air. It was the wealthy who had access to credit. This gave them extra purchasing power. It switched resources from the subsistence goods of the working man to the sophisticated commodities of the rich. Shelley saw credit as the worker's enemy, because it expanded the sphere of money, dragging the worker away from his cottage into the horror of the milltowns, to depend on the whims of the market. He points down a road that attracted many of the later poets (as well as Marx). Defoe saw credit as the worker's friend because it fostered growth and full employment, the conventional view that underpins the economy as we know it. Yet Shelley had a point. Printing money creates winners (mainly the rich) and losers (mainly the poor), as happened on a vast scale after the financial crash of 2007-2008.

Under the traditional system, anybody with a £5 note could convert it on demand into its equivalent in gold. During the Napoleonic Wars the Government suspended the 'convertibility' of the currency, to protect the national gold reserves. In 1820 Britain still had a paper currency, which Shelley saw as a playground for unscrupulous parasites:

> The existing government of England, in substituting a currency of paper for one of gold, has had no need to depreciate the currency by alloying the coin of the country; they have merely fabricated pieces of paper on which they promise to pay a certain sum … Of this nature are all such transactions of companies and banks as consist in the circulation of promissory notes to a greater amount than the actual property possessed by those whose names they bear. They have the effect of augmenting the prices of provision, and of benefiting at the expense of the community the speculators in this traffic. One of the vaunted

> effects of this system is to increase the national
> industry, that is, to increase the labours of the poor
> and those luxuries of the rich which they supply

The alternative to a paper currency was one convertible into gold on request. This was the 'gold standard' of financial markets. When Britain restored the gold standard in 1821 prices fell, causing a recession. This benefited lenders, such as Shelley's hated rentiers, at the expense of borrowers and workers. In the long run the gold standard strengthened the nation's finances. As other countries adopted it, Britain's financial power spread across the globe. Shelley would have hated all this and was an unlikely supporter of the gold standard. *Queen Mab* suggests a different view of gold:

> Commerce has set the mark of selfishness,
> The signet of its all-enslaving power,
> Upon a shining ore, and called it gold;
> Before whose image bow the vulgar great,
> The vainly rich, the miserable proud,
> The mob of peasants, nobles, priests and kings,
> And with blind feelings reverence the power
> That grinds them to the dust of misery.

In condemning the paper currency Shelley was harking back to a more innocent age. He saw the disruptive power of credit: how the tide of new money had empowered an enterprising minority, uprooted an old way of life, pushed an army of desperate people into the mills and enriched some unsavoury parasites in the process. The end result was to devalue the labour of the poor, their only property. He must have seen that credit could not be uninvented. Doing away with it would have caused a massive slump. His programme was meant to avoid a revolution by offering real change. He singled out the national debt for reform. It was clear:

> — That the majority of the people of England are destitute and miserable, ill-clothed, ill-fed, ill-educated.
> — That they know this, and that they are impatient to procure a reform of the cause of this abject and wretched state.
> — That the cause of this misery is the unequal distribution which, under the form of the national debt, has been surreptitiously made of the products of their labour and the products of the labour of their ancestors; for all property is the produce of labour.

The debt should be abolished, whether outright or through a levy on the rich:

> If the principal of this debt were paid, it would be the rich who alone could, and justly they ought to pay it. It would be a mere transfer among persons of property.

Shelley could claim support from Adam Smith, no less,

for insisting that wars should be financed from taxation, not borrowing. In *The Wealth of Nations*, Smith called the national debt a *pernicious* system of funding. It encouraged governments to pursue military adventures overseas, and fostered jingoism among the public who, untroubled by having to pay for the war:

> enjoy at their ease, the amusement of reading in the newspapers the exploits of their own fleets and armies … They are commonly dissatisfied with the return of peace, which puts an end to their amusement, and to a thousand visionary hopes of conquest and national glory.

Adam Smith would probably have suggested abolishing import duties on foreign grain, as an obvious way to lower the price of bread. This would have given immediate relief to the poor at the expense of landowners (instead, the duties were increased with the Corn Laws of 1815). Shelley had a different scheme. *Queen Mab* includes a note on the many political and economic benefits, if the nation were to adopt a vegetarian diet:

> The change which would be produced by simpler habits on political economy is sufficiently remarkable. … The quantity of nutritious vegetable matter, consumed in fattening the carcase of an ox, would afford ten times the sustenance … if gathered immediately from the bosom of the earth. The most fertile districts of the habitable globe are

now actually cultivated by men for animals, at a delay and waste of aliment absolutely incapable of calculation. It is only the wealthy that can, to any great degree, even now, indulge the unnatural craving for dead flesh …

The spirit of the nation that should take the lead in this great reform would insensibly become agricultural; commerce, with all its vice, selfishness, and corruption, would gradually decline; more natural habits would produce gentler manners, and the excessive complication of political relations would be so far simplified … How would England, for example, depend on the caprices of foreign rulers if she contained within herself all the necessaries, and despised whatever they possessed of the luxuries, of life? How could they starve her into compliance with their views? Of what consequence would it be that they refused to take her woollen manufactures, when large and fertile tracts of the island ceased to be allotted to the waste of pasturage?

Much of this is now accepted wisdom. Two thirds of global agricultural land is devoted to feeding livestock (and 1% to pet food!). Eating so much meat adds to global warming, leaves us dependent on foreign grain, harms our health and rests on industrial farming methods which do us no credit.

Shelley also believed in free love. He had clearly read

Malthus' *Essay on Population* and took the strongest ex-
ception to it. Malthus was a priest who wrote on demo-
graphy and economics. He started from the premise
that food supply grew arithmetically while population
grew geometrically. Population must therefore be kept
in check, to match the food supply. This would either
happen through disease, hunger war and vice; or through
sexual abstinence by the poor. The *Essay* was a great edi-
fice of logic piled up on simple assumptions which turned
out to be wrong. But not before it had inspired some
very hard-hearted theories and policies. Hence Shelley's
invective:*

* The criticism was understandable but Malthus was not all bad. There
were passages in the *Essay on Population* that Shelley might have agreed
with, eg. that rearing beef makes corn scarcer for the poor, or that:

> The consumable commodities of silks, laces, trinkets, and expen-
> sive furniture, are undoubtedly a part of the revenue of the society;
> but they are the revenue only of the rich, and not of the society in
> general. An increase in this part of the revenue of a state, cannot,
> therefore, be considered of the same importance as an increase of
> food, which forms the principal revenue of the great mass of the
> people.

His book also influenced Darwin as he worked on the theory of evolu-
tion, a reason to be grateful. In economics, Malthus foresaw that a slump
could occur due to a lack of demand (as did Coleridge — see p. 78).
Orthodoxy still denied this in the 1930s. Keynes in a biographical essay
of 1933 maintained that:

> the almost total obliteration of Malthus's line of approach and
> the complete domination of Ricardo's for a period of a hundred
> years has been a disaster to the progress of economics. Time after
> time… Malthus is talking plain sense, which Ricardo, with his
> head in the clouds, wholly fails to comprehend.

A writer of the present day (a priest of course, for his doctrines are those of a eunuch and of a tyrant) has stated that the evils of the poor arise from an excess of population, and after they have been stript naked by the tax-gatherer and reduced to bread and tea and fourteen hours of hard labour by their masters … He has the hardened insolence to propose as a remedy that the poor should be compelled … to abstain from sexual intercourse, while the rich are to be permitted to add as many mouths to consume the products of the labours of the poor as they please.

When the poor were told to abstain from sex on the say-so of a mathematical formula, things had gone too far. The social sciences were there to serve society, not dictate to it:

Whilst the mechanist abridges, and the political economist combines labour, let them beware that their speculations, for want of correspondence with those first principles which belong to the imagination, do not tend, as they have in modern England, to exasperate at once the extremes of luxury and want. They have exemplified the saying, 'To him that hath, more shall be given; and from him that hath not, the little that he hath shall be taken away.' The rich have become richer, and the poor have become poorer; and the vessel of the State is driven between the Scylla and

Charybdis of anarchy and despotism. Such are the effects which must ever flow from an unmitigated exercise of the calculating faculty.

This warning comes from *A Defence of Poetry* which ends with the famous phrase:

Poets are ... the mirrors of the gigantic shadows which futurity casts upon the present; the words which express what they understand not; the trumpets which sing to battle and feel not what they inspire; the influence which is moved not, but moves. Poets are the unacknowledged legislators of the world.

This graph perhaps suggests one of those *gigantic shadows which futurity casts upon the present*. It shows how average living standards barely changed from antiquity until the industrial revolution; and then multiplied fifty-fold over the next two hundred years. Shelley stood at that extraordinary turning point and seems to have felt, with deep unease, a gathering force that was to change the face of the earth.

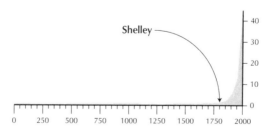

Estimates of global GDP per person, 0-2000 AD (Bank of England)

SAMUEL TAYLOR COLERIDGE
1772-1834

*A long and attentive observation has convinced me
that formerly men were worse than their principles
but that at present the principles are worse
than the men.*

A LAY SERMON

The author of *Kubla Khan* and *The Rime of the Ancient
Mariner*, a poet-philosopher steeped in German meta-
physics, was not an obvious authority on taxes. But there
was another side to Coleridge. He had been secretary to
the Governor of Malta; he had friends in business; the
radical student had become a middle aged conservative;
and he had taken to journalism after running out of
money.

The Friend was a weekly review, entirely written by
Coleridge. As a business venture it was doomed. Coleridge
was then living in the Lake District with Wordsworth.
His copy was sent across the mountains to Penrith where
it was printed, then posted to a list of subscribers. Each
issue consisted of a long essay by Coleridge, usually on a
literary or philosophical theme, with a poem or two as a
bonus. Against all odds, Coleridge managed twenty eight

issues in the space of ten months. *Vulgar Errors Respecting Taxes and Taxation* was No. 12. It appeared in November 1809, during the Napoleonic wars.

Peace was nowhere in sight. The cost of the war was much resented. Coleridge, who supported the war, wanted to show that it was affordable. A nation's debts were owed to itself, like *a husband and wife playing cards at the same table against each other, where what the one loses the other gains.* Money raised in taxes continued to circulate in the economy where it could do much good, if wisely spent:

> The Gardens in the South of Europe supply [an] illustration of a system of Finance, judiciously conducted, where the tanks or reservoirs would represent the Capital of a Nation, and the hundred rills, hourly varying their channels and directions under the Gardener's Spade, give a pleasing image of the dispersion of that capital through the whole population, by the joint effect of Taxation and Trade.

Napoleon had all the resources of continental Europe at his disposal, but they were no match for Britain's financial system. Coleridge imagined the national debt as an oxygen pump, mobilising the whole country with fresh supplies of credit:

> every pulse in the Metropolis produces a correspondent pulsation in the remotest Village … the

cause and Mother Principle of this unexampled Confidence, of this system of Credit, which is as much stronger than mere positive possessions as the Soul of Man is than his Body ... the main cause of this, I say, has been our NATIONAL DEBT.

There followed some rather modern thoughts on credit creation. By stimulating inflation, monetary growth forced people to put their capital to work or see it fritter away (part of the thinking behind inflation targets, now set by most central banks). New business ventures offered new ways for people to invest their money, leading to new financial surpluses and fresh investment – and so to a virtuous circle:

> It is the National Debt which, by the rapid nominal rise in the value of Things, has made it impossible for any considerable number of Men to retain their own former comforts without joining in the common industry and adding to the Stock of national Produce; which thus first necessitates a general activity, and then, by the immediate and ample Credit, which is never wanting to him who has any object on which his activity can employ itself, gives each Man the means not only of preserving but of increasing and multiplying all his former enjoyments.

The tax burden was easily sustainable thanks to years of economic growth:

the actual labour and produce of the country has not only been decupled within half a century but increased so prodigiously beyond that decuple as to make 600 millions a less weight to us than 50 millions were to our grandfathers.

Coleridge had no doubt that this growth flowed from *that system of credit and paper currency of which the national debt is the reservoir and water works*. It was another hundred years before economists began to picture the economy as a circular flow and created hydraulic models to show how it worked. Coleridge seems to hint at the 'multiplier effect', the discovery by Keynes and others in the 1930s that money injected into the economy in effect grows as it continues to circulate around the system. The multiplier can also work in reverse. Coleridge argued that abolishing the credit system would mean less money in circulation. Activity would dry up – a catastrophe, not least for the poor:

Neither could it be the Labourer's interest: for he must be either thrown out of employ, and lie like the Fish in the Bed of a River from which the water has been diverted, or have the value of his labour reduced to nothing, by the irruption of eager Competitors.

As a bonus, for readers who persevered to the end of *Vulgar Errors*, there were some aphorisms, including this dig at the enemy over the Channel:

For a French House Dog's Collar
When Thieves come I bark; when Gallants, I am still
So perform both my Master's and Mistress's Will.

To most economists, war was the ultimate destroyer of wealth. J. S. Mill, perhaps with *Vulgar Errors* in mind, described Coleridge as an *arrant driveller* in political economy. De Quincey called Coleridge's economic views *chimeras*, but ones based on serious study:

> Coleridge did not, like Wordsworth, dismiss political economy from his notice disdainfully, as a puerile tissue of truisms or of falsehood not less obvious, but actually addressed himself to the subject; fancied he had made discoveries in the science; and even promised us a systematic work on its whole compass.
>
> *Recollections of the Lakes and the Lake Poets,* 1839

If Coleridge ever planned such a book he must have changed his mind. He moved to Highgate in 1816, to undergo treatment for his opium addiction as an in-patient with Dr Gillman. He proved unreliable as a patient but so interesting as a guest that he stayed for the rest of his life. The 'Sage of Highgate' now emerged as a spokesman for a more caring form of conservatism. It came wrapped up as a lecture on ethical reasoning, addressed to a governing class forgetful of Plato and the Bible. *The Statesman's Manual, or the Bible, the Best Guide to Political Skill and Foresight* flew far above the heads of its audience. The

obscurity was heroic but the message was more or less
discernible. A society based only on *Mechanic understand-
ing* was doomed. The true guide to value was *Reason*, an
overall view of life based on philosophy and religion. As
to political economy:

> in its zeal for the increase of food, it habitually
> overlooked the qualities and even the sensations
> of those that were to feed on it. As ethical philos-
> ophy, it recognised no duties which it could not
> reduce into debtor and creditor accounts on the
> ledgers of self-love ... it has dearly purchased a few
> brilliant inventions at the loss of all communion
> with life and the spirit of nature.

In 1817 Coleridge returned to the charge with *A Lay
Sermon Addressed to the Higher and Middle Classes on the
Existing Distresses and Discontents*. The rather portentous
title hid a less obscure work with more to say about polit-
ical economy. Its main thrust was to blame Britain's woes
on an *overbalance of the commercial spirit*. Commerce was
important but had to be matched by other forces – by a
wise ruling class with non-commercial values, by philoso-
phy and by religion. All three were on the wane, allowing
the *spirit of trade* to get out of control:

> We are – and, till its good purposes, which are
> many, have all been achieved, and we can become
> something better, long may we continue such! –
> a busy, enterprising and commercial nation. The

habits attached to this character must, if there is
no adequate counterpoise, inevitably lead us, un-
der the specious names of utility, practical knowl-
edge and so forth, to look at all things through the
medium of the market, and to estimate the worth
of all pursuits and attainments by their marketable
value. In this does the spirit of trade consist.*

The *Lay Sermon* was also an attempt to explain the
post-war slump, and to offer some rather novel ideas for
curing it. Taxation was no threat to the economy so long
as the money went straight back into circulation. At a
time when most wealth was inherited by people who did
no work, Coleridge thought government spending could
stimulate growth by taking from the idle rentier and
spending with the go-ahead maker or merchant (part of
the classsic case for taxes on unearned income). The econ-
omy would benefit both from the government spending
and from:

> the check which taxation, in its own nature,
> gives to the indolence of the wealthy in its con-
> tinual transfer of property to the industrious and

* Capitalism needs stable institutions and respect for ethical norms such
as honesty. Joseph Schumpeter (the famous economist, a champion of
capitalism) shared Coleridge's concern in his *Capitalism, Socialism and
Democracy* (1942):

> In breaking down the pre-capitalist framework of society, capital-
> ism thus broke not only the barriers that impeded its progress but
> also the flying buttresses that prevented its collapse.

enterprising. … The settlement of the amount will be in favour of the national wealth, to the amount of all the additional productive labour sustained or excited by the taxes during the period between their efflux and their re-absorption.

The immediate cause of the post-war slump was a sudden drop in government spending. Soldiers and sailors were released *en masse* back onto the labour market, just as demand for military equipment dried up. In short, peace had produced a major demand shock, made worse by similar slumps in Britain's trading partners:

these again, in their reaction, are sure to be more than doubled by the still greater and universal alarm, and by the consequent check of confidence and enterprise.

The idea that government spending could expand or contract the economy, working through the level of overall demand, seems to foreshadow Keynes. Distinguished economists still disagree about taxes and public spending, as about most things. For the rest of us, perhaps the safest lesson is that people's economics usually follow from their politics. Shelley opposed the war, Coleridge supported it and each found economic arguments to bolster his position.

Among the symptoms of the *spirit of trade* Coleridge identified a regular cycle of boom and bust, driven by speculative excess in the financial markets:

Within the last sixty years … there have occurred at intervals of about twelve or thirteen years each, certain periodical revolutions of credit … I ought to have said gradual expansions of credit ending in sudden contractions or … ascensions to a certain utmost possible height, which has been different in each successive instance; but in every instance the attainment of this, its *nec plus ultra*, has been instantly announced by a rapid series of explosions (in mercantile language, a crash) and a consequent precipitation of the general system.

For a short time this Icarian credit … this illegitimate offspring of confidence … seems to lie stunned by the fall; but soon recovering, again it strives upward … alarm and suspicion gradually diminish into a judicious circumspectness; but by little and little circumspection gives way to the desire and emulous ambition of doing business; till impatience and incaution on one side, tempting and encouraging headlong adventure, want of principle, and confederacies of false credit on the other, the movements of trade become yearly gayer and giddier, and end at length in a vortex of hopes and hazards, of blinding passions and blind practices which should have been left, where alone they ought ever to have been found, among the wicked lunacies of the gaming table.

The flight and fall of 'Icarian Credit' foreshadows the

cycle described in the 1960s by the economist Hyman Minsky, though largely ignored until a 'Minsky moment' hit the world in 2007 (Coleridge would find Icarian credit alive and well – perhaps he would have foreseen the crash). The excesses of Icarian Credit perverted the financial system and led to periodic slumps in the real economy. These slumps did great social harm which economists then glossed over as 'adjusting' to a new level:

> We shall perhaps be told too, that the very Evils of this system, even the periodical crash itself, are to be regarded but as so much superfluous steam ejected by the escape pipes and safety valves of a self-regulating machine: and lastly, that in a free and trading country *all things find their level* …
>
> But persons are not things – but man does not find his level! After hard and calamitous season, during which the thousand wheels of some vast manufactory had remained silent as a frozen water-fall, be it that plenty has returned and that trade has once more become brisk and stirring: go ask the overseer, and question the parish doctor, whether the workman's health and temperance … have found *their* level again.

Unjust policies, such as the Highland Clearances, were all too often justified by the technocrats of the day with utilitarian arguments based on 'the greatest good for the greatest number'. Coleridge was having none of it.

Here he recalls a conversation with an old lady in the
Highlands, a victim of the Clearances, who might have
stepped out of a novel by Walter Scott:

> Within this space – how short a time back! – there
> lived a hundred and seventy three persons; and
> now, there is only a shepherd and an underling or
> two. Yes Sir! ... Christian Souls, man, woman, boy,
> girl and babe, an old man by the fireside ... and
> many a brave youth among them who loved the
> birthplace of his forefathers yet would swing about
> his broad-sword and want but a word to march off
> to battle ... Well, but they are gone ... and with
> them the potato-plot that looked as gay any flower
> garden ... And do you think Sir, that God allows
> of such proceedings?
>
> I was sometime after told by a very sensible
> person who had studied the mysteries of political
> economy ... that more food was produced in
> consequence of this revolution, that the mutton
> must be eat somewhere, and what difference
> where? If three were fed at Manchester instead
> of two at Glencoe or the Trosachs, the balance of
> human enjoyment was in favour of the former.
> I have passed through many a manufacturing
> town since then, and have watched many a group
> of old and young, male and female, going to or
> returning from many a factory, but I could never
> yet persuade myself to be of his opinion. Men, I

still think, ought to be weighed not counted. Their
worth ought to be the final estimate of their value.

Coleridge had lived in the countryside and knew
it well. As a young man he mostly travelled on foot.
Farming was both the backbone of the economy and
an age-old way of life. Land was originally given to the
gentry in return for feudal service. As Coleridge saw it,
the gentry held their land in trust from the Crown and
should follow the *aims of the State* in their dealings with all
who lived and worked on their estates. Those aims were:

1. To make the means of subsistence more easy to
each individual;

2. To secure to each of its members the hope of
bettering his own condition, or that of his chil-
dren;

3. The development of those faculties which are
essential to his humanity, that is, to his rational
and moral being.

In short, landowners should act in a paternal spirit, with
an eye not to profit but to *a healthy, callous-handed but
high and warm-hearted tenantry.* Coleridge showed that
commercial principles led to the consolidation of farms
into ever larger units, with the fewest labourers, the larg-
est marketable output and the least share kept back to
feed the villagers themselves. It was in these areas that
people most relied on the Poor Laws:

> in agricultural districts three quarters of the poor
> rates are paid to healthy, robust and (Oh sorrow
> and shame!) industrious hard-working paupers in
> lieu of wages (for men cannot at once work and
> starve) … the poor laws are a subject I should not
> undertake without trembling … this enormous
> mischief is undeniably the offspring of the com-
> mercial system.

At the time, farm wages were kept as low as possible
but topped up by the parish, just enough to avoid star-
vation. Defenders of the system suggested that low wages
and large farms made for cheap food, which made in turn
for a plentiful and cheap industrial workforce, able to
compete in markets overseas. Coleridge denied that any
of this was necessary. It came from *the commercial spirit
un-counteracted and unenlightened* and had created:

> a state of things so remote from the simplicity of
> nature, that we have almost deprived Heaven it-
> self of the power of blessing us; a state in which,
> without absurdity, a superabundant harvest can be
> complained of as an evil, and the recurrence of the
> same a ruinous calamity.

In the days when a leading economist could write
with authority about a poet, J. S. Mill devoted a forty
page essay to Coleridge, praising him (despite the 'drivel-
ler' jibe) for providing a necessary antidote to the cruder
sort of utilitarianism, and especially for

reviving the idea of a *trust* inherent in landed property. The land, the gift of nature, the source of subsistence to all, the foundation of everything that influences our physical well-being, cannot be considered a subject of property in the same absolute sense.

Coleridge had no time for Shelley's brand of radical politics. In *A Lay Sermon*, he saw markets as a force for good. *To buy in cheapest and sell in dearest market is a legitimate maxim of trade*. (Or, as he put it in a later essay, business was one of the *forces of progression*.) He seemed to accept that in following their self-interest businessmen could also serve the general interest, like the shopkeepers who made sure there was always food to buy:

> Even so is it with the capitalists and storekeepers who, by spreading the dearness of provisions over a larger space and time, prevent scarcity from becoming real famine, the frightful lot at certain and not distant intervals of our less commercial forefathers. These men, by the mere instinct of self interest, are not alone birds of warning that prevent waste, but, as the raven of Elijah,* they bring supplies from afar.

Laissez-faire and the 'laws' of political economy were another matter. Human beings were not to be treated as

---

* 1 Kings 17. God arranged for the ravens to feed Elijah while in hiding.

variables in some cold utilitarian calculus. As a poet and philosopher, Coleridge appealed to the *Intellectual responsibility of the upper classes* :

> If you possess more than is necessary for your own wants, more than your own wants ought to be felt by you as your own interests.

He expected reform to come from the voluntary efforts of an enlightened governing class. The rights of property might be sacred and the duties of the State limited, but they did include the duty to stop private property from trespassing on the State's own *inalienable and untransferable property – I mean the health, strength, honesty and filial love of its children.* These four duties were a test which the governing class duly failed. In 1815 Parliament began considering limits on child labour. It was proposed to ban the employment of children under ten, and limit older children to ten hours work a day. There was fierce opposition. The Bill would be a gift to competitors overseas; it would undermine laissez-faire and interfere with the freedom of contract; children were better off in the mills; their parents needed the money… Coleridge had seen similar arguments trotted out in defence of slavery. He demolished them in a series of pamphlets:

> But *free* Labour! – in what sense not utterly sophistical, can the labour of children, extorted from the wants of their parents, 'their poverty but not their

will consenting'* be called '*free*'? … the common
result of the present system of labour in the cotton
factories is disease of the most painful and wasting
kind, and too often a premature death … if the
labour were indeed free, the employer would pur-
chase, and the labourer sell, what the former had no
right to buy, and the latter no right to dispose of;
namely, the labourer's health, life and well-being.

Arguments based on laissez-faire were pure hypocrisy.
Parliament was happy to interfere with property rights
when it suited the rich, as when they wanted to enclose
the common land or build a canal:

Every canal Bill shows that there is no species of
property which the legislature does not possess
and exercise the right of controlling and limiting,
as soon as the right of the individuals is shown to
be disproportionately injurious to the community.

The Factory Bill would eventually pass in 1819, in
watered down form, the minimum age reduced to nine,
with no inspectorate, applying only to the cotton mills,
and so forth. Arguments supposedly drawn from political
economy were brandished in brazen support of vested in-
terests. All this confirmed Coleridge in his dislike of the
subject. In a letter of 1818 he wrote:

I have been doing my best on behalf of the poor

* *Romeo and Juliet*, Act V, line 75

Cotton Factory Children whose condition is an abomination which has weighed on my feelings from earliest manhood ... I dare affirm, that few superstitions in Religion have been so extensively pernicious to the intellectual and moral sanity of this country and France, as those of (so called) Political Economy ... It is a science which begins with *abstractions* in order to exclude whatever is not subject to technical calculations: in the face of all experience, it assumes these as the *whole* of human nature – and then, on an impossible hypothesis, builds up the most inhuman edifice, a Temple of Tescalipoca!*

Whenever it suits the interests of the Rich, *i.e.* their imaginary interests, not as men but as Rich, they can then discover that it is, like geometry, an abstract science, from which in practice all sorts of deviations must be allowed ... but when morals, health humanity plead – O! they are then inviolable truths. Free labour must not be interfered with &c.

Coleridge denied that land or labour could be subject to free market forces alone. There are premonitions here of Karl Polanyi's *The Great Transformation*, one of the seminal books to come out of the Second World War. Polanyi distinguished between 'real' commodities, things

* An Aztec god, worshipped with human sacrifice

produced to be sold in the market like food or clothes; and 'fictitious' commodities, notably land, labour and capital, the three classic factors of production. Men and women cannot be a commodity. Nor can land, which belongs to the very fabric of society. Capital and credit are social constructs, dependent on trust as well as law. They are also far too powerful and open to abuse to be simply let rip. Polanyi showed that society always pushes back against a free market in 'fictitious' commodities; and that only a managed version of capitalism can survive without destroying the social fabric on which it depends.

Coleridge might agree with much of this. Some of his economic ideas were well ahead of their time. But it would be a stretch to claim him as a forefather of the modern mixed economy. He would, more likely, deplore our godless consumer society; and link our environmental catastrophe to a gross *overbalance of the commercial spirit.* He told his readers that a better society would follow when its leaders became *better people.* By this he meant people who centred their lives not on profit and loss alone but on the deeper truths of nature, philosophy and religion:

> the intuition of ultimate principles ...These alone can interest the undegraded human spirit deeply and enduringly, because these alone belong to its essence and will remain with it permanently.
>
> *The Statesman's Manual*

SIR WALTER SCOTT
1771-1832

*In the fluctuations of mercantile speculation, there is
something captivating to the adventurer, even inde-
pendent of the hope of gain. He who embarks on that
fickle sea, requires to possess the skill of the pilot and
the fortitude of the navigator, and after all may be
wrecked and lost, unless the gales of fortune breathe in
his favour … trade has all the fascination
of gambling without its moral guilt.*

ROB ROY

Every note issued by the Bank of Scotland bears the
image of Sir Walter Scott, the saviour of the Scottish
banknote.

It happened in 1826. Private banks in those days could
issue their own notes. After several English banks col-
lapsed, leaving worthless notes in circulation, the Gov-
ernment decided to ban private banknotes smaller than
£5 – then a substantial sum. This would have left gold
and silver coins as the currency for most smaller transac-
tions. London had overlooked the implications for Scot-
land, where people relied on small notes for their daily
business. The reform was a grave threat to Scotland's

economy, especially in remote areas where gold and silver were rarely found.

Early 1826 found Walter Scott at a low ebb: in chronic pain, his wife dying and his fortune in ruins. His publishers had recently collapsed, leaving him liable for £130,000 as a partner in the firm. Bankruptcy was the cheapest option but Scott insisted on working off the debt, as a matter of honour. It was a daunting task – a debt worth tens of millions in today's money – though not impossible for the most popular author in Europe. A cynic might wonder if Scott's campaign against the banking reform was a return for the banks' forbearance. His private journal shows the opposite. The banks were nervous of provoking the authorities in London. Scott joined the fight as a Scottish patriot.

Negotiations over Scott's debt reached a low point on 16 February. He was almost ready to give up and go bankrupt. On the same day he began to think of campaigning against the bank reform. Two days later he set to work on the first *Letter of Malachi Malagrowther* (a pen name, taken from one of his novels – there was no doubt about the real author):

FEBRUARY 18. —

I set about Malachi Malagrowther's Letter on the late disposition to change everything in Scotland to an English model, but without resolving about the publication. They do treat us very provokingly.

'Land of Cakes!' said the Northern bard,
'Though all the world betrays thee,
One faithful pen thy rights shall guard,
One faithful harp shall praise thee.'

A press article was ready the next day. It caused an encouraging stir. Within a few days Scott had worked it up into a full-length pamphlet:

FEBRUARY 23. —

The pamphlet will soon be out — meantime Malachi prospers and excites much attention. The Banks have bespoke 500 copies. The country is taking the alarm; and I think the Ministers will not dare to press the measure … I do believe Scotsmen will show themselves unanimous at least where their cash is concerned. They shall not want backing …

Whimsical enough that when I was trying to animate Scotland against the currency bill, John Gibson brought me the deed of trust, assigning my whole estate to be subscribed by me; so that I am turning patriot, and taking charge of the affairs of the country, on the very day I was proclaiming myself incapable of managing my own … Who would think of their own trumpery debts, when they are taking the support of the whole system of Scottish banking on their shoulders?

Despite his debts Scott was well qualified to fight the

bank reform. As a successful lawyer he understood the issue. As an acclaimed poet and novelist he was sure of an audience. As Walter Scott he could speak for a nation still deeply divided, eighty years after the Jacobite rebellion of 1745. In real life he was a lowlander: sheriff, lawyer, land-owner, friend to the high and mighty in London. But in his imagination he was often a highlander: the creator of Rob Roy, Flora McIvor and other highland heroes.

Malagrowther's first message was political: the English should mind their own business. Under the Treaty of Union, Scotland had the right to manage her own affairs. The banking reform was unconstitutional. The Chancellor of the Exchequer had foisted his reform on Scotland out of a perverse desire for uniformity. The legal arguments were sugared with a typical Scott anecdote. It is set in the castle of Glamis, where the old Earl of Strathmore used to insist on perfect symmetry between the two sides of his garden, just like the English with their banking reform:

> It chanced once upon a time that a fellow was caught committing some petty theft, and, being taken in the manner, was sentenced ... to stand for a certain time in the baronial pillory, called the *jougs*, being a collar and chain, one of which contrivances was attached to each side of the portal of the great avenue which led to the castle. The thief was turned over accordingly to the gardener as ground-officer, to see the punishment duly

inflicted. When the Thane of Glamis returned from his morning ride, he was surprised to find both sides of the gateway accommodated each with a prisoner, like a pair of heraldic supporters chained and collared proper. He asked the gardener, whom he found watching the place of punishment, as his duty required, whether another delinquent had been detected. 'No, my Lord,' said the gardener, in the tone of a man excellently well satisfied with himself, 'but I thought the single fellow looked very awkward standing on one side of the gate-way, so I gave half-a-crown to one of the labourers to stand on the other side for uniformity's sake.' This is exactly a case in point.

Malagrowther's economic message was equally simple: Scotland's banks suited Scotland's needs. They had brought new life to far-flung, impoverished regions:

> Through means of the credit which this system has afforded, roads have been made, bridges built, and canals dug … in the most sequestered districts of the country, manufactures have been established, unequalled in extent or success – wastes have been converted into productive farms … let those who remember Scotland forty years since bear witness if I speak truth or falsehood.

Bank failures were rare in Scotland. The banks carefully policed each others' credit, since they were obliged to accept each other's notes. If a bank left the stony paths of virtue this was soon picked up by their central clearing house in Edinburgh (an *Argus eyed tribunal*). The banks' shareholders usually included a wide range of local land-owners and merchants. Their capital base was solid, their structure sound, their aims and conduct worthy:

> The bankers of Scotland have been, general-ly speaking, *good* men, in the mercantile phrase, showing by the wealtha of which they have died possessed, that their credit was sound; and *good* men also, many of them eminently so, in the more extensive and better sense of the word, manifest-ing, by the excellence of their character, the fairness of the means by which their riches were acquired.

Malachi Malagrowther appeared in the middle of a serious economic slump (which had brought on Scott's own bankruptcy). In difficult times the banks had stood by their customers – the contrast with our own times is painful – and had

> come forward to support the tottering credit of the commercial world with a frankness which au-gured the most perfect confidence in their own resources.

Along with credit, local banks brought peace, good order and falling crime. With cash safely held in the bank, there was far less robbery:

Look at the old magazines or newspapers, during the time when the currency was chiefly maintained by specie,* a ready temptation to the ruffian ... the murder of graziers and dealers returning from fairs where they had sold their cattle, was a not infrequent occurrence. Farm-houses of the better class, as well as gentlemen's baronial residences, were defended by bars on the windows, upper and under, like those of a prison; yet these houses were often broken open by daring gangs, to possess themselves of the hoards which the tenant must have then kept beside him against rent day, and his landlord, for the current expense of his household.

Profit from their banknote business allowed local banks to pay interest on the smallest deposits. This was a spur to thrift and hard work. The banking reform would discourage regular habits among the working people:

The first motive to save, among petty tradesmen, mechanics, farm-servants, domestics, and the like, is the delight of forming a productive capital; and in that class, the habit of saving and of frugality is the foundation of a sober, well-regulated, and useful society. Every judicious farmer scruples to repose perfect reliance in a farm-servant or a labourer, till he knows that he is possessed of a capital of a few pounds in some neighbouring bank;

* Specie = gold or silver coins

and when that is once attained, the man becomes tenfold steady and trustworthy.

What is a poor hind or shepherd to do with his £20 or £30, the laborious earnings of his life, and which he looks to, under God, for keeping his widow and family from the parish, if bankers can no longer afford him some interest for the use of it? Where is he to get decent security for his petty capital? He will either be swindled out of it by some rascally attorney, or coaxed to part with it to some needy relation, in either case never to see it more.

Above all, the banks had brought new life to the poorest parts of the Kingdom. Thanks to them, catching and curing herring, once a Dutch monopoly, had finally taken hold in Scotland. Without the banks, both fishing and 'kelping' (turning sea weed into soda-ash) would collapse:

The branches of … the Scottish Banks, maintained at convenient and centrical points in the north of Scotland, furnish all the remote and numerous stations where the fisheries are carried on, with small notes and silver for payment of the actual fisher's labour, and in return accept the bills of the fish-curers upon the consignees …

The manufacture of Kelp, which is carried on to an immense extent through all the shores and isles of the Highlands, supporting thousands of

men with their families, who must otherwise emi-
grate or starve, and forming the principal revenue
of many Highland proprietors, is nearly, if not ex-
actly, on the same footing with the fisheries ; is
carried on chiefly by the same medium of circula-
tion ; and, like them, supplied by the Bankers with
small notes for that purpose, at a reasonable profit
to themselves, and with the utmost advantage to
the country and its productive resources.

Let any man who knows the country, or
will otherwise endeavour to conceive its pover-
ty and sterility, imagine if he can, the difficul-
ties, expense, and hazard, at which gold must
be carried to points where it would never have
voluntarily circulated, and from whence, un-
less detained in some miser's hoard ... it will
return to London with the celerity of a carrier-
pigeon.

Scott's financial ruin had brought many offers of help
and sympathy. These only added to the humiliation.
With *Malachi Malagrowther*, he felt in charge again. The
old roar was back. A second pamphlet went to the print-
ers, timed for a big public meeting:

MARCH 3. —

It is ridiculous enough for me, in a state of insol-
vency for the present, to be battling about gold
and paper currency. It is something like the hu-

morous touch in Hogarth's Distressed Poet, where
the poor starveling of the Muses is engaged, when
in the abyss of poverty, in writing an Essay on
payment of the National Debt; and his wall is
adorned with a plan of the mines of Peru. Never-
theless, even these fugitive attempts, from the suc-
cess which they have had, and the noise they are
making, serve to show the truth of the old proverb
—

> When house and land are gone and spent,
> Then learning is most excellent.

On the whole, I am glad of this brulzie, as far as
I am concerned; people will not dare talk of me
as an object of pity — no more 'poor-manning'.
Who asks how many punds Scott the old champi-
on had in his pocket when

> He set a bugle to his mouth,
> And blew so loud and shrill,
> The trees in greenwood shook thereat,
> Sae loud rang ilka hill?

In his final letter Malagrowther imagines himself in
dialogue with his neighbour Christopher Crystal, a dealer
in silver knick-knacks and a keen supporter of economic
orthodoxy:

'Why, Mr Malachi Malagrowther,' said my friend,
in wrath, 'I pronounce you ignorant of the most

ordinary principles of Political Economy' ... Here
he raised his voice, as if speaking *ex cathedra*. 'Gold,'
continued he, '... like all other commodities, will
flow to the place where there is a demand for it. It
will be found, assure yourself, wherever it is most
wanted; ... it is the demand that makes the supply,
and so it will be with the gold ... those fishing and
kelping operations are not productive – are use-
less to the country ... they only occasion the mis-
employment of so much capital, the loss of so much
labour ... Send your Highland fishers to America
and Botany Bay, where they will find plenty of food
and let them leave their present sterile residence in
the untamed undisturbed solitude for which Na-
ture designed it. Do not think you do any hardship
in obeying the universal law of nature, which lead
wants and supplies to draw to their just and proper
level ... sweep out of your head ... all that absurd
rubbish of ancient tradition ... we look to what
is USEFUL sir, and to what is useful only; and
our March towards utility is not to be interrupted
by reference to antiquated treaties or obsolete pre-
judices'.

Once he has recovered from this imaginary onslaught,
Malagrowther replies that Scotland's gold flows not
northwards to the highlands but southwards to London.
The Scots paid £4m a year for the pleasure of being ad-
ministered from Whitehall and further huge sums to ab-

sentee landlords, living in the fleshpots of England. There was a constant drain on the local money supply:

> A metaphor is no argument … Scotland, sir, is not beneath the level to which gold flows naturally. She is above it and she may perish ere she sees a guinea … metallic currency has a natural tendency to escape from a poor country back to a rich one. Just so, a man might die of thirst on top of a Scottish hill, though a river lay at the base of it.

The image of things 'finding their level' was an abstraction of the sort dear to economists, which skated over the human cost of the adjustment process. Importing gold to serve as currency would impose an extra cost on the poorest areas. It would cripple their fledgling industries:

> The Scottish fisheries … are already supporting themselves, and producing a moderate but certain profit; only that this profit is as yet so moderate that it will certainly not bear an impost of probably five or six per cent upon the gross capital employed … It is the highest impolicy to smother by such a burden, important national undertakings … It would be like breaking the reed ere it had attained its strength.

There follows an eloquent case for a regional economic policies of the sort that are now commonplace:

Secondly, Admitting, from the great poverty of the inhabitants, and other discouraging circumstances, that the Scottish fisheries have for a long time required the support of Government, I still aver, that the expense attending such support has been well and wisely disposed of … An exotic shrub, when first planted, must be watered and cared for, a child requires tenderness and indulgence till he has got through the sickly and helpless years of infancy. A fishery or manufacture, established in a wild country, and among a population of indolent habits, unaccustomed to industry, and to the enjoyment of the profits derived from it, will, at the outset, require assistance from the State, till old habits are surmounted, and difficulties overcome.

In the present case, the Government has done this duty amply – the tree has taken root … the fisheries are in full progress to triumphant success … Thriving villages are already to be found where there were scarcely to be seen the most wretched hovels; a population lazy and indolent, because they had no motive for exertion, have become, on finding the employment and tasting the fruits of industry, an enterprising and hardy race of seamen, well qualified to enrich their country in peace – to defend her in time of war.

And finally, a plea to put people above dogma:

> Lastly, I would say a word in behalf of the peo-
> ple of Scotland, merely as human beings … Even
> if departing the kelpers would somehow create a
> greater gain in England, consider first the char-
> acter of the population you are about to consign
> thus summarily … Poor as the inhabitants are,
> the wants of the Highlanders are limited to their
> circumstances; and they have enjoyments which
> make amends, in their own way of reckoning,
> for deprivations which they do not greatly feel
> … every heart must feel some sympathy when I
> say, they love their country, rude as it is, because it
> holds the churches where their fathers worshipped
> and the churchyards where their bones are laid.

As a young man, Scott once met Adam Smith. He
later recorded the event:*

> we shall never forget one particular evening, when
> he put an elderly lady, who presided at the tea ta-
> ble, to sore confusion, by neglecting utterly her in-
> vitation to be seated, and walking round the circle
> stopping ever and anon to steal a lump from the
> sugar basin, which the venerable spinster was at
> length constrained to place on her own knees, as

---

* In *The Life and Works of John Home*, a biographical sketch of the play-
wright, who knew Smith well. Scott was nineteen when Adam Smith
died in 1790.

the only method of securing it from his most un-
economical depradations.

Adam Smith was notoriously absent-minded. Scott
added a story about Smith's arrival one day at the Ed-
inburgh Customs-House when he noticed, for the first
time, the porter's ceremonial salute:

> This ceremony must have been performed before
> the great Economist perhaps five hundred times.
> Nevertheless one day … and on a sudden, he be-
> gan to imitate his gestures, as a recruit does those
> of a drill sergeant. The porter, having drawn up
> in front of the door, presented his staff as a sol-
> dier does his musket; the commissioner, raising his
> cane, and holding it with both hands by the mid-
> dle, returned the salute with the utmost gravity …
> The functionary, much out of countenance, next
> moved up the stairs, with his staff advanced, while
> the author of *The Wealth of Nations* followed with
> his bamboo in precisely the same posture …
>
> … but whoever has read the deep theories and
> abstruse calculations contained in *The Wealth of
> Nations* must readily allow that a mind habitual-
> ly employed in such themes, must necessarily be
> often rapt far above the sublunary occurrences of
> everyday life.

Adam Smith was in reality a man of the world. He
spent a year escorting the teenage Duke of Buccleuch on

a grand tour of Europe, mingling as easily with princes as professors. The views which Scott puts into the mouth of Christopher Crystal are a caricature of utilitarian thinking, to which Smith's successors were prone. Smith himself, writing fifty years earlier, came to much the same conclusion as Malagrowther about the value of the Scottish banks:

> The business of the country is almost entirely carried on by means of the paper of those different banking companies, with which purchases and payments of all kinds are commonly made. Silver very seldom appears … and gold still seldomer. But though the conduct of all those different companies has not been unexceptionable … the country, notwithstanding, has evidently derived great benefit from their trade. I have heard it asserted, that the trade of the city of Glasgow, doubled in about fifteen years after the first erection of the banks there; and that the trade of Scotland has more than quadrupled since the first erection of the two public banks at Edinburgh.
>
> *Wealth of Nations,* 1776

Distrust of political economy came naturally to Scott. The conservative, the romantic and the sceptical lawyer all rebelled against a system of thought that managed to be both cold and thoroughly disruptive:

Here you have a pamphlet – there a fishing town.

Here the long continued prosperity of a whole nation — and there the opinion of a professor of Economics, that in such circumstances she ought not to have prospered at all … if you are determined, like Æsop's dog, to snap at the shadow and lose the substance, you never had such a gratuitous opportunity of exchanging food and wealth for moonshine in the water.

Three months after Scott picked up his pen the banking reform was dead. Triumph came with sadness. As he turned to his journal with a final word on the victory, his beloved Charlotte was fading away:

MAY 13. —

The projected measure against the Scottish banknotes has been abandoned, the resistance being general. Malachi might clap his wings upon this, but, alas! domestic anxiety has cut his comb.

Scott's message boils down to this: everyone needs access to decent, affordable financial services. Running them is a sacred trust, not a licence to gamble. Probity is the backbone of finance. He had taken foolish risks, tried to cut corners and ended up near-bankrupt. But he learned his lesson and set out to make amends, working on through pain and bereavement until the debts were eventually cleared (though he did not live to see it). Scott would be no fan of today's banks: their hubris a big cause of the financial crash; surviving only because 'too big to fail'; rescued by the taxpayer yet still generating scandals, like the misselling of insurance policies worth tens of billions of pounds. Scott had trenchant views on speculators and 'financial engineers' of every sort:

> fishers in troubled waters, capitalists who sought gain not by the encouragement of fair trade and honest industry, but by affording temporary fuel to rashness or avarice ... Such reptiles have been confined in Scotland to batten upon their proper prey of Folly and waste, like worms on the corruption in which they are bred.

THOMAS DE QUINCEY
1785-1859

A crazy maxim has got possession of the whole world,
viz. *that price is, or can be, determined by the*
relation between supply and demand.
THE LOGIC OF POLITICAL ECONOMY

The *Confessions of an English Opium Eater* tell how Thomas de Quincey became addicted to the drug. While semi-comatose from its effects he stumbled on Ricardo's *Principles of Political Economy and Taxation.* This produced an epiphany:

> In this state of imbecility I had, for amusement, turned my attention to political economy; my understanding, which formerly had been as active and restless as a hyæna, could not, I suppose (so long as I lived at all) sink into utter lethargy ... Great as was the prostration of my powers at this time, yet I could not [but] ... be aware of the utter feebleness of the main herd of modern economists ... I saw that these were generally the very dregs and rinsings of the human intellect ...

> At length, in 1819, a friend in Edinburgh sent
> me down Mr. Ricardo's book ... I said, before I
> had finished the first chapter, 'Thou art the man!'
> Wonder and curiosity were emotions that had
> long been dead in me.

By sheer force of logic, Ricardo had uncovered a crys-
talline scientific structure beneath the outward random-
ness of economic life. He had:

> deduced *a priori*, from the understanding itself,
> laws which first gave a ray of light into the un-
> wieldy chaos of materials, and had constructed
> what had been but a collection of tentative dis-
> cussions into a science of regular proportions, now
> first standing on an eternal basis.

However, De Quincey detected some flaws in Ricar-
do's logic. These he set about correcting:

> Thus did one single work of a profound under-
> standing avail to give me a pleasure and an activity
> which I had not known for years. It roused me
> even to write ... I drew up my Prolegomena to
> all future Systems of Political Economy.* I hope
> it will not be found redolent of opium; though,
> indeed, to most people the subject is a sufficient
> opiate.

* Which was written but never published.

Until this episode De Quincey had been a poet *man-qué*. As a teenager he sent one of the first fan letters Wordsworth ever received. To meet Wordsworth became the central object of his life. A few years later he succeeeded, becoming part of Wordsworth's circle. In due course he took over Dove Cottage (now the central Wordsworth shrine), when the poet moved to a larger house. Coleridge was next among De Quincey's idols – he once sent Coleridge an anonymous gift of £300 (part of a small inheritance which soon ran out). These friendships were never easy. They finally broke down over De Quincey's splendidly candid memoir, *Recollections of the Lake Poets*.

Opium was then available from any chemist, generally mixed with alcohol as laudanum. De Quincey first took it to relieve a migraine but stayed with it for pleasure:

> the opium-eater ... feels that the diviner part of his
> nature is paramount; that is, the moral affections
> are in a state of cloudless serenity, and over all is
> the great light of the majestic intellect.

He later became addicted after overdosing to relieve a chronic stomach pain. This was a legacy from a time of great hardship, spent on the run from school. He was saved from dying of cold and hunger by the kindness of 'Ann', a fifteen-year-old prostitute who afterwards haunted his opium fevers. All this, together with his pæan to Ricardo, was recounted in the *Confessions,* which first appeared in 1821.

David Ricardo was one of Shelley's *pelting wretches*: he made enough money from stockbroking to buy Gatcombe Park – now home to Princess Anne – with 5,000 acres of land. His *Principles* have had a vast impact. His theory of comparative advantage provides the intellectual underpinning of free trade and thus of globalisation. Ricardo's work was remorseless in logic, cold and dry but had a metaphysical side that de Quincey much enjoyed. Like Adam Smith, Ricardo thought labour was the correct measure of value. But he refined the theory:

> The value of a commodity, or the quantity of any other commodity for which it will exchange, depends on the relative quantity of labour which is necessary for its production.

Everything had a *primary and natural price* based on its labour content. Market prices were a *deviation* from these natural prices, due to temporary gaps between supply and demand. The job of market prices was to pull resources from one trade to another until the natural order was restored. It must have seemed obvious to men reared on Plato that everything should have a 'natural' or underlying value, more significant than its ever-shifting market price.

De Quincey, with his fluent classical Greek and mastery of Aristotelian logic, revelled in such complications. *The Templars' Dialogues* (1824) were an attempt to bolster Ricardo's theory of value. They amount to a

tortuous ninety page rumination on the 'natural' value
of de Quincey's hat. This turned out to be measured by
the *amount* of labour that went into its making (Ricardo's
view), which was on no account to be confused with the
value of that labour (Adam Smith). Finding this 'natural'
value was the key problem in economics, although the
answer had little bearing on the hat's market price. As De
Quincey warned, in his main economic treatise, *The Logic
of Political Economy* (1844):

> it is a great aggravation of the other difficulties in
> the science of Economy that the most metaphysi-
> cal part comes first.

De Quincey liked to flavour his theorising with out-
landish examples. To have 'value in exchange' a thing
had to have both an 'intrinsic utility' which De Quincey
called U; and a 'difficulty of attainment', called D. Both
had to be present before one or the other could operate in
practice. To illustrate U – intrinsic utility, or how badly
somebody really wants something – De Quincey whisked
the reader off to Canada:

> You are on Lake Superior in a steamboat, making
> your way to an unsettled region 800 miles ahead
> of civilisation, and … with no chance at all of pur-
> chasing any luxury whatever … for a space of ten
> years to come. One fellow passenger, whom you
> will part with before sunset, has a powerful musi-
> cal snuffbox; knowing by experience the power of

such a toy over your own feelings … you are vehe-
mently desirous to purchase it … But the owner,
aware of your situation, is determined to operate
by a strain pushed to the very uttermost upon U,
upon the intrinsic worth of the article in your in-
dividual estimate.

In this example 'you' ended up paying £60 for a snuff-
box costing £6 to make. Perhaps 'snuffbox' was a code-
word for opium. De Quincey was at pains to stress that U
had everything to do with desire and nothing to do with
'usefulness':

the use contemplated is the simple power of min-
istering to a purpose, though that purpose were
the most absurd, wicked, or destructive to the user
that could be imagined.

U only applied to rare or very special goods, like the
first rhinoceros ever imported, in the reign of Charles II,
which fetched £2000 (then a fortune). Such goods sold
for whatever the highest bidder would pay. Ordinary
goods that could be reproduced at will – or for which
there were plenty of substitutes – were priced according
to their 'difficulty of attainment' or D. This was simply
the cost of producing them:

Enter the slave market at Constantinople … as it
existed at the opening of this nineteenth century.
The great majority of ordinary slaves were valued

simply as effects … They had been stolen; and the cost of fitting out a similar foray when divided suppose amongst a thousand captives, quoted the price of each ordinary slave. …

There might be slight variations even among rank and file slaves, based on their health, age etc. But in the main … the mob, the plebs , among the slaves, must be valued as the small ordinary pearls are valued …

But the natural aristocracy among slaves, like the rarer pearls, will be valued on other principles. Those who were stolen from the terraces and valleys lying … between the Euxine and the Caspian had many chances … of proving partially beautiful … Amongst the males, some would have a Mameluke value, as promising equestrian followers in battle, as capital shots, as veterinary surgeons, as soothsayers or calculators of horoscopes.

And if we could go back to the old slave markets of the Romans, we should meet a range of prices (corresponding to a range of accomplishments) as much more extensive as the Roman civilisation was itself nobler and ampler … Generally no doubt, the learned and the intellectual slaves … such as Tiro, the private secretary of Cicero, were vernal slaves … home bred descendants of slaves imported in some past generation, and trained at their master's expense upon any promise of talent.

> Tutors, physicians, poets, actors ... architects and
> artists of all classes, *savants littérateurs* – nay some-
> times philosophers not to be sneezed at – were to
> be purchased in the Roman markets.
>
> And this, by the way, was undoubtedly the
> cause of that somewhat barbarian contempt which
> the Romans, in the midst of a particular refine-
> ment, never disguised for showy accomplishments.

De Quincey added that the rising price of slaves
was one reason for Cæsar's British expeditions. He then
turned to what are now called 'positional goods' – things
whose supply is essentially fixed, such as period homes,
or places at top universities. If such goods become widely
available, they lose their point.* De Quincey cites *Popish
reliques* to prove that positional goods lose their magic as
soon as they are mass produced:

> Even a Saint can have only one cranium; and in
> fact the too great multiplication of these relics, as
> derived from one and the same individual saint
> or martyr was one of the causes, cooperating with
> changes in the temper of society ... which grad-
> ually destroyed the market in relics ... when ...
> the King of France led by the bridle the mule who
> bore such relics, and went on foot, bare headed,

---

* Fred Hirsch, in *Social Limits to Growth* (1976) explains how the general
striving for positional goods, which motivates much of our economic
activity, is bound to end in disappointment for most of us.

to meet them — these were great spiritual powers
… This was their affirmative value, and when that
languished, they could not pass over to the other
scale of negative value … for they could not be
openly reproduced.

De Quincey denied that prices were, or could be, set
by the interplay of supply and demand. In a perfectly com-
petitive market, prices were set at their 'natural' level,
which relected labour content. A gap between supply and
demand could push a price off its natural level. It then
became a 'market price' which was unnatural, or 'adfect-
ed'. 'Natural' and 'market' prices were *two poles of a law*,
whereas an actual price, or 'price in a market', was a mere
fact. There was, however, something a bit shady about
unnatural prices:

shoemakers are notoriously such philosophic men,
and the demand of the public is so equable, that
no man buys shoes or boots at any than the steady
natural price. The result of this difference is seen
in the two orders of men, shoemakers and horse
dealers … Mr Coleridge and many others have
declared the shoemaker's craft to be the most prac-
tically productive of meditation among men. This
has partly been ascribed to its sedentary habits; but
much more I believe depends upon the shoemak-
er's selling always at natural, never at unnatural or
market prices; whilst the unhappy horse dealer,

being still up to his lips in adfected price, and ab-
solutely compelled to tamper with this price, nat-
urally gets the habit of tampering with the buyer's
ignorance, or any other circumstance that shapes
the price to his wishes.

If one substitutes *estate agent* for *horse dealer*, a cer-
tain sense begins to emerge. Cobblers are also becoming
a thing of the past, thanks to factory made trainers, and
shoes at a *steady natural price* now seem a distant dream.

The *Logic of Political Economy* appeared in 1844. De
Quincey was nearing sixty, a widower with five surviv-
ing children. But in money matters he was still the half-
starved 'opium eater', never far from the financial abyss.
He was often on the run from his creditors, holed up
in some hidden garret. At such times the children had
to smuggle copy to his publishers, through the streets of
Edinburgh, while keeping house, as best they could, at
the far end of the city. De Quincey had rubbed shoulders
with earls and broken bread with beggars. He knew soci-
ety from both ends and had no illusions about its brutal
underside; as he says in the *Confessions*:

> it cannot be denied that the outside air and
> framework of London society is harsh, cruel, and
> repulsive.

Yet he seemed to delight in the established order. In
this pæan to the London banker, De Quincey explains
how capital flows from trade to trade and from country to

country, in search of greater profit. Whole communities may be left stranded when a new industry supplants an old one, but capital moves smoothly on:

> in silent arches of continual transition, ebbing and flowing like tides, do the re-agencies of the capital accumulated in London modify, without sound or echo, much commerce in all parts of the world. Faithful to the monetary symptoms and the fluctuations this way or that eternally perceptible in the condition of every trade, the great monied capitalist, standing at the centre of this enormous web, throws over his arch of capital or withdraws it, with the precision of a fireman directing columns of water from an engine upon the remotest corner of a conflagration …
>
> Not a man has shifted from his station; … yet power and virtue have been thrown into vast laboratories of trade, like shells into a city. But all has been accomplished in one night, by the inaudible agency of the post office … Such is the perfection of our civilisation.

There are traces here of Coleridge, with his *hundred rills, hourly varying their channels and directions under the Gardener's Spade* — but the spirit has changed. Where Coleridge was genial, De Quincey's image seems menacing. He had every sympathy for the poor as individuals but none at all as a class. The Peterloo massacre found him firmly on the side of authority. Likewise, the Anti-Corn Law League were a group of *pernicious agitators*, out to stir up the British working man. Abolishing the Corn Laws would do nothing for the poor, destroy British agriculture and drive up the cost of food in corn exporting countries. Nor did he have much truck with foreigners. The opium wars should be conducted with *exemplary vigour*: how dare the Chinese close their ports to British opium runners? Moral objections to the war were pure hypocrisy. The Chinese were merely protecting their own opium growers.

> China is incapable of a true civilisation, semi-refined in manners and mechanic arts but incurably savage in the moral sense.

As for Ireland, the country was entirely to blame for its own woes: *the luxury of excessive indolence had, from the earliest period, fascinated Ireland into a savage life*, while the advent of the potato had made this idleness compatible with *a vast expansion of the population*.

For a man with such views, at least one of Ricardo's theories had dangerous implications. Economists generally disapprove of rent, a polite word for unearned income. Ricardo was no exception. In the *Principles* he described land rents as:

> that portion of the produce of the earth which is paid to the landlord for the use of the original and indestructible powers of the soil.

Ricardo's theory of rent suggested that landowners would scoop all the gains from economic growth. As rising demand for corn pushed up its price, farmers would boost supply by bringing less fertile land into cultivation. They would make higher profits on the more fertile land but this would allow landowners to increase rents. Tenant farmers, those who actually grew the crops, would be no better off. Nor would their workers: wages would rise but so would food prices. De Quincey was worried. By implication the landowners were dangerous parasites. Ricardo's logic pointed to a looming crisis:

> Our own social system seems to harbour within itself the germ of our ruin. Either we must destroy rent … or rent will destroy us, unless in the one sole case where this destroying agency can be headed back.

However all was not lost. First, high rents were a symptom not a cause of high corn prices. Prices were based on the cost of cultivating the least fertile ('marginal') acre of land. But rent at the 'margin' was zero and zero rents could not be responsible for anything.* More importantly, rent could indeed be 'headed back'. Ricardo had built a tower of logic on a bed of faulty assumptions (a habit often known as the 'Ricardian vice'). De Quincey

---

* A fine piece of casuistry since rents still come out of the poor man's loaf. De Quincey took it from Ricardo. The theory was long-lived. It gave Bernard Shaw apoplexies — see p. 165.

correctly forecast that new techniques and discoveries would keep farm output growing in step with population. This growth in productivity would allow profits and wages to keep pace with rents. The landowners' share would stay much the same:

> Only through the great antagonist force for ever at work in Great Britain – through skill, capital, and the energy of freemen; only by an antagonist law for ever operative in throwing back the descents … Thus, and only thus, do we escape, have escaped, and shall escape, the action of rent.

De Quincey became an apologist for the rich and powerful. He was proud to have saved them from:

> a dreadful class of systematic enemies to property … a wild ferocious instinct, blind as a Cyclops and strong as a Cyclops.

The rich gave him little thanks and left him on the breadline, where he seemed at home. He had no interest in wealth or possessions, apart from books, and no desire for material progress. Quite the contrary. A rich inner life was becoming impossible in the speed and bustle of 1845 Britain:

> unless this colossal pace of advance can be retarded (a thing not to be expected), or, which is happily more probable, can be met by counter forces of corresponding magnitude, forces in the direction

of religion or profound philosophy ... the natural
tendency of so chaotic a tumult must be to evil;
for some minds to lunacy, for others to a regency
of fleshly torpor ... No man ever will unfold the
capacities of his own intellect who does not at least
checker his life with solitude.

Suspiria de Profundis

Many other romantics ended up as Tories, dismayed
with the ugliness and upheaval of industrial society ('con-
servatives' generally identified with the landed interest;
'pro-business' conservatism still lay in the future). De
Quincey managed to blend romantic high-Toryism with
a fascination for Ricardo, a liberal champion of free trade.
He came to economics as an exercise in logic, a soothing
distraction from the pains of opium. The logic came first,
even before Tory polemics.

In this spirit, De Quincey rejected Malthus' fore-
cast that population was bound to grow faster than
food supplies. In logic, there was no link between the
two (as many others had pointed out, food reproduc-
es far faster than humans). Yet he strongly agreed with
Malthus that it was futile, even wicked, to spend mon-
ey on benefits for the poor. The Poor Laws, he wrote
in an article on Malthus, had an *obvious tendency to
degrade the moral character of their objects in their best
elements of civic respectability*. It was a classic attack on
'benefit-scroungers'.

The opium and the *Confessions* have made De Quincey

a modernist icon, admired by writers from Baudelaire to Borges. Yet he paid for the opium by airing robustly conservative views in a vast output of magazine articles, on subjects from China to the Corn Laws. Their length and learning belong to another age; but the use of economics as a sort of cosh, the jingoism and general provocative gusto must make De Quincey one of the forefathers of British tabloid journalism.

JOHN RUSKIN

1819-1900

*The following pages contain, I believe, the first
accurate analysis of the laws of Political Economy
which has been published in England.*

MUNERA PULVERIS

Film-goers know John Ruskin as a preachy Victorian
obsessive who failed to consummate his marriage.
There must be more to a man whose work was revered
by Tolstoy and Gandhi. If he had never written a line, he
would be remembered for beautifully observed watercol-
ours and drawings. But he took to art history and became
famous with *Modern Painters,* a brave book in praise of
contemporary artists. With *The Stones of Venice,* he be-
came a major celebrity. The book is studded with prose
poems of stately splendour. It gripped the imagination of
Victorian Britain.

Ruskin came to political economy through the study
of art. In the buildings of Venice, he could survey a thou-
sand years of history. He admired gothic buildings above
all others. Their lack of uniformity and 'polish' gave them
a mysterious power. No two columns were identical.

Medieval craftsmen had licence to vary and embellish: their carving came from the soul. During the Renaissance wealthy patrons turned to the *pernicious* classical style, with its cold symmetry. There was no more need for the craftsman's soul, only his obedience to plan. The descent had begun towards the misery of the modern industrial worker, matched by the spiritual decline of the ruling class.

The Wealth of Nations begins with the division of labour, which Adam Smith saw as opening the road to material progress. Smith was troubled, all the same, by its human cost; Ruskin was appalled by it. *The Nature of Gothic** is, among other things, a broadside against an industrial system based on *the degradation of the operative into a machine,* in which workers were made to feel *less than men*:

> We have much studied and perfected of late, the great civilised invention of the division of labour; only we give it a false name. It is not, truly speaking, the labour which is divided but the men:
> – Divided into mere segments of men – broken into small fragments and crumbs of life …
>
> And the great cry that rises from all our manufacturing cities, louder than their furnace blast, is … that we manufacture everything there except men; we blanch cotton, and strengthen steel, and

* By far the best-known chapter in *The Stones of Venice.*

refine sugar, and shape pottery but to brighten,
to strengthen, to refine or to form a single living
spirit, never enters into our estimate of advantages.

Consumers were complicit in the misery of workers,
like the tourists who bought glass beads, produced in ap-
palling conditions on the Venetian Island of Murano. It
was their duty to forego *such convenience... or cheapness as
is to be got only by the degradation of the workman*; and to
buy only the products of *healthy and ennobling labour*.

William Morris later published *The Nature of Gothic*
as a socialist tract, though Ruskin defies such labels, see-
ing himself as both *a violent Tory of the old school* and *a
Communist, reddest of the red*. His best known economic
work, *Unto this Last* (1860), is an attack on the methods,
values and assumptions of political economy, a *mass-de-
lusion* built around an 'economic man' who did not exist
and a complete misunderstanding of how society works:

> The social affections, says the economist, are acci-
> dental and disturbing elements in human nature;
> but avarice and the desire of progress are constant
> elements. Let us eliminate the inconstant, and,
> considering the human being merely as a covetous
> machine, examine by what laws of labour, pur-
> chase and sale the greatest accumulative result in
> wealth is obtainable.

Since they built on false foundations, economists
could only come to false conclusions. They had no

useful advice to give, for instance on the decade-long slump then gripping the economy:

> at a severe crisis, when lives in multitudes, and wealth in masses, are at stake, the political economists are helpless—practically mute; no demonstrable solution of the difficulty can be given by them, such as may convince or calm the opposing parties.

People were not motivated by money alone. Crude utilitarianism – the *balance of expediency* – was a hopeless guide to social conduct. Society rested on basic notions of justice. The proper aim of policy was to seek the *balance of justice*. For instance, the just policy on wages was to fix them, and at a fair level:

> … for all the important, and much of the unimportant, labour on the earth, wages are already so regulated.
>
> We do not sell our prime-ministership by Dutch auction; nor, on the decease of a bishop … do we (yet) offer his diocese to the clergyman who will take the episcopacy at the lowest contract. … The natural and right system respecting all labour is, that it should be paid at a fixed rate, but the good workman employed, and the bad workmen unemployed. The false, unnatural, and destructive system is when the bad workman is allowed to offer his work at half-price, and either take the place

of the good, or force him by his competition to work for an inadequate sum.

Ruskin's father was a successful sherry merchant who lived in style and left his son a fortune. In return Ruskin was rather condescending towards his father. He would be astonished that modern business managers earn so much for a job requiring, in his view, such modest skills:

> the … tact, foresight, decision and other mental powers required for the successful management of a large mercantile concern … would at least match the general conditions of mind required in the subordinate officers of a ship … or in the curate of a country parish.

Businessmen were held in generally low repute because they were *presumed to act always selfishly*. The public were merely taking businessmen at their own word. If they wanted respect they should put their customers and their craft ahead of profit. As the soldier's profession was to defend the nation, so the merchant's duty was to provide for it:

> it is no more his function to get profit for himself out of that provision than it is a clergyman's function to get his stipend.

Profit was an adjunct to doing a good job, that is, producing the very best goods at the fairest possible price; while taking the fullest care for the workforce. Ruskin anticipated 'stakeholder capitalism': it was good advice, which might have spared us such recent horrors as Grenfell Tower, Dieselgate or the sight of brand-new jets, full of passengers, falling from the sky. With wealth came responsibility. Employers should share the hard times and lead from the front:

> And as the captain of a ship is bound to be the last man to leave his ship in case of wreck, and to share his last crust with the sailors in case of famine, so the manufacturer, in any commercial crisis or distress, is bound to take the suffering of it with his men, … as a father would in a famine, shipwreck, or battle, sacrifice himself for his son.

Money and wealth were not the same thing. Money, like electricity, needed a negative as well as a positive pole. Its power depended on others' need for it:

> What is really desired, under the name of riches, is essentially, power over men … the art of becoming 'rich', in the common sense, is not … finally, the art of accumulating much money for ourselves, but also of contriving that our neighbours shall have less. In accurate terms, it is the art of establishing the maximum inequality in our own favour.

With his High Tory side, Ruskin had nothing against inequality. But wealth based on injustice was another matter:

The whole question, therefore, respecting not only the advantage, but even the quantity, of national wealth, resolves itself finally into one of abstract justice. It is impossible to conclude, of any given mass of acquired wealth, merely by the fact of its existence, whether it signifies good or evil to the nation [it] may be indicative, on the one hand, of faithful industries, progressive energies, and productive ingenuities; or, on the other ... of mortal luxury, merciless tyranny, ruinous chicane.

The condition of the people was the true measure of wealth (this may seem a truism but reformers are still trying to translate the idea into practice, for instance by replacing growth with 'wellness' as the aim of policy). So long as growth and profit were the guiding stars, economists would suggest lowering wages to 'stay competitive' or 'restore equilibrium'. This, said Ruskin, was the very opposite of wealth:

Since the essence of wealth consists in power over men, will it not follow that the nobler and the more in number the persons are over whom it has power, the greater the wealth? ... that the final outcome and consummation of all wealth is in the producing as many as possible full-breathed, bright-eyed, and happy-hearted human creatures.

Our modern wealth, I think, has rather a tendency the other way;—most political economists

appearing to consider multitudes of human crea-
tures not conducive to wealth, or at best conducive
to it only by remaining in a dim-eyed and narrow-
chested state of being.

Victorian economists saw labour as the best yardstick
of 'value'. One thing would exchange for another that
represented the same amount of labour. This was a gift
to a moralist like Ruskin. How then should the reward of
labour be fixed? Certainly not by the play of demand and
supply. If labour was the source of value then an hour's
labour should be rewarded with an equivalent command
over the labour of others:

> If we promise to give him less labour than he has
> given us, we under-pay him. If we promise to give
> him more labour than he has given us, we over-
> pay him. In practice, according to the laws of de-
> mand and supply, when two men are ready to do
> the work, and only one man wants to have it done,
> the two men under-bid each other for it; and the
> one who gets it to do, is under-paid.

Formulas based on demand and supply overlook the
massive imbalance of power that so often exists between
buyer and seller. Coleridge made the same point about
child labour. The labour market was heavily tilted to-
wards the employer because workers were desperate. The
outcome was often tantamount to theft, as a worker's la-
bour was his only property:

whereas it has long been known that the poor have
no right to the property of the rich, I wish it also
to be known ... that the rich have no right to the
property of the poor.

It was not possible to establish an exactly just wage
because it was hard to compare the value of different sorts
of labour. But it was better to agree a roughly fair wage by
applying principles of justice than to reach a scientifical-
ly unfair one through the strife of competitive bidding.
Men should not be made to undercut each other in a race
to the bottom:

I want a horseshoe for my horse. Twenty smiths or
twenty thousand ... may be ready to forge it; their
number does not in one atom's weight affect the
question of the equitable payment of the one who
does forge it.

By contrast, the reigning orthodoxy maintained that
wages could never rise for long above a minimum sub-
sistence level. As Ricardo wrote in *The Principles of Political
Economy and Taxation* (1817):

Labour, like all other things which are purchased
and sold, and which may be increased or dimin-
ished in quantity, has its natural and its market
price. The natural price of labour is that price
which is necessary to enable the labourers, one
with another, to subsist and to perpetuate their
race, without either increase or diminution.

This was later dubbed the 'Iron Law of Wages'. It was another classic example of the 'Ricardian vice' – logic built on shaky assumptions (see p. 119) – but it was widely believed and had chilling implications for the real world. It led to a widespread belief that miserable wages were a fact of life, sanctioned by the laws of economics. Ruskin made hay with this:

> Ricardo, with his usual inaccuracy, defines what he calls the 'natural rate of wages' as 'that which will maintain the labourer.' Maintain him! yes; but how?—the question was instantly thus asked of me by a working girl, to whom I read the passage. I will amplify her question for her. 'Maintain him, how?' As, first, to what length of life? Out of a given number of fed persons how many are to be old—how many young; that is to say, will you arrange their maintenance so as to kill them early—say at thirty or thirty-five on the average, including deaths of weakly or ill-fed children?—or so as to enable them to live out a natural life? … which does Mr. Ricardo mean to be their natural state, and to which state belongs the natural rate of wages?

If nothing else, Ruskin showed that economic 'laws' which seem unjust or counter-intuitive can and should be challenged. Ricardo's whole apparatus of natural prices was eventually dropped.

Ruskin looked for intrinsic qualities, not numbers. Wealth was either built on wise choices or it was built on sand:

> All wealth is intrinsic … many things which are true wealth in moderate use, yet become false wealth in immoderate … to receive pleasure from an evil thing is not to escape from, or alter the evil of it, but to be altered by it … nothing, but harm ever comes of a bad thing.
>
> So that, finally, wealth is not the accidental object of a morbid desire, but the constant object of a legitimate one.

This led on to the idea of *illth*, perhaps Ruskin's most famous insight. It is a commonplace that much of our 'wealth' comes with a downside. Plastic bags, fast fashion, betting shops, tanning parlours – much of we count as wealth is arguably the opposite, or 'illth'. Ruskin applied the term to our behaviour as much as to things. Wine was good in moderation, bad in excess. 'Wealth' meant good things in wise hands:

> if a thing is to be useful, it must be not only of an availing nature but in availing hands. Or, in accurate terms, usefulness is value in the hands of the valiant …
>
> Wealth is therefore 'THE POSSESSION OF THE VALUABLE BY THE VALIANT' …

> Whence it appears that many of the persons commonly considered wealthy, are in reality no more wealthy than the locks of their own strong boxes are; they being inherently and eternally incapable of wealth; and operating for the nation, in an economical point of view, either as pools of dead water, and eddies in a stream … acting, not as wealth, but … as 'illth', causing various devastation and trouble around them in all directions.

One of the many odd conclusions of classical economics was a belief that, as J. S. Mill put it, *Saving … enriches, and spending impoverishes.* Spending on non-essentials was believed to reduce the 'wages fund' – the amount of money employers had left to pay their workers. A smaller 'wages fund' meant less employment and lower output (Mill later abandoned the doctrine). Ruskin, though no friend of luxury, thought wise consumption was the whole purpose:

> For as consumption is the end and aim of production, so life is the end and aim of consumption. The final object of political economy, therefore, is to get good method of consumption and great quantity of consumption; in other words, to use everything and to use it nobly …
>
> THERE IS NO WEALTH BUT LIFE. Life, including all its powers of love, of joy and of admiration. That country is the richest which numbers

the greatest number of noble and happy human beings; that man is richest who, having perfected the functions of his own life to the utmost, has also the widest influence, both personal and by means of his possessions, over the lives of others.

Ruskin's central message is that we are not just consumers in a market. If we are truly to prosper, we must act as members of society, indeed heirs to a civilisation, held in trust for future generations. To forget this is to open a gulf between what the market values and what is real value; and this can have disastrous consequences for society, as for the environment. He was early into the field of green economics. In *The Crown of Wild Olive* he pictures Carshalton (now a busy London suburb). Streams that once ran pure and clear are now polluted with:

> foulness, heaps of dust and slime, broken shreds of old metal, and rags of putrid clothes … Half a dozen men with one days' work could cleanse those pools … But that day's work is never given, nor, I suppose, will be.

On the other hand, a nearby pub had installed a hideous set of iron railings, making it harder to sweep behind them. It prompted Ruskin to a description of 'market failure', the idea that markets find it easier to provide 'illth', which usually has a price ticket, than to provide valued amenities, such as clean air or parks, which do not:

> Now the iron bars which, uselessly enclosed this
> bit of ground and made it pestilent, represented a
> quantity of work which would have cleansed the
> Carshalton pools three times over; of work partly
> cramped and perilous in the mine; partly grievous
> and horrible, at the furnace; partly foolish and sed-
> entary, of ill-taught students making bad designs
> … how did come to pass that this work was done
> instead of the other? … There is but one reason for
> it … that the capitalist can charge percentage on
> the work in the one case, and cannot in the other.

He saw that the true costs of industry were largely
neglected by economists. He was one of the first to de-
scribe atmospheric pollution and he warned in lurid
tones of its dangers:

> everywhere, and all day long, you are vitiating it
> with foul chemical exhalations; and the horrible
> nests, which you call towns, are little more than
> laboratories for the distillation into heaven of ven-
> omous smokes and smells, mixed with effluvia
> from decaying animal matter, and infectious mi-
> asmata from purulent disease.

Ruskin took the common sense view that money in-
fluenced the real economy of goods and services. Money
was dangerous because it could be accumulated *ad in-
finitum*, merely for its own sake, with no real purpose
in mind. Yet the business of accumulation necessarily

skewed the real economy, usually for the worse. Money was thus the essential enabler of a modern economy, with its restless growth and never-ending new wants: :

> Three fourths of the demands existing in the world are romantic; founded on visions, idealisms, hopes and affections; and the regulation of the purse is, in its essence, regulation of the imagination and the heart.*

The subject is covered more fully in *Munera Pulveris*, Ruskin's most systematic work on political economy. He distinguished between 'store-holders', who treasured their possessions (with money merely a means to obtain them); and 'currency holders' who treasured money for its own sake (things being merely a means to show off their 'wealth'). He had only scorn for the latter:

> The large currency-holder himself is essentially a person who never has been able to make up his

---

* Colin Campbell has pinned the blame for these boundless appetites on the romantic movement itself. In his famous book *The Romantic Ethic and the Spirit of Modern Consumerism* (1987), he says that the insatiable wanting of the modern consumer is unique. All other cultures have shared much the same limited range of needs and social activities. Only when the romantics freed the modern imagination to roam, was our own culture able to transcend these traditional limits. Modern desires are limited only by the imagination; they propel the modern economic model in its quest for endless growth. Whether or not the romantics are to blame, they would, of course, deplore the way things have turned out.

mind as to what he will have, and proceeds, there-
fore, in vague collection and aggregation, with
more and more infuriate passion, urged by com-
placency in progress, vacancy in idea, and pride
of conquest.

Here Ruskin predicts that finance will grow ever larger
compared to the real economy (as indeed has happened):

In proportion as the habits of the nation become
complex and fantastic … its circulating medium
must increase in proportion to its store. If every-
one wants a little of everything- if food must be of
many kinds, and dress of many fashions- if mul-
titudes live by work which, ministering to fancy,
has its pay measured by fancy … and worst of all,
if the currency itself, from its largeness, and the
power which the possession of it implies, becomes
the sole object of desire with large numbers of the
nation … in all these cases, the currency necessari-
ly enlarges in proportion to the store … and as an
object of passion, has a more and more important
and malignant power over the nation's dealings,
character, and life.

Ruskin thought gold currency was a *barbarism — a
remnant of the conditions of barter … among savage na-
tions.* He also came to believe that any form of interest on
loans was usury and therefore *unnatural and impious.* It
was not only on usury that Ruskin looked to the Middle

Ages. He came to reject the whole apparatus of free markets, believing that in society, as in the arts:

> Government and cooperation are in all things the
> Laws of Life; Anarchy and competition the Laws
> of Death.

As ever, he was not content with preaching. He poured effort and money into his Guild of Saint George, designed to spread these ideals in practice. He foresaw a guild system on medieval lines that would replace competition with regulation in all branches of the economy:

> all the master bakers in a town … are not to try to
> undersell each other, nor seek each to get the oth-
> er's business, but are all to form one society, selling
> to the public under a common law of severe pen-
> alty for unjust dealing, and at an established price.

Goods would all be made to an approved quality and standard, policed by the relevant guild:

> and this fixing of standard would necessitate much
> simplicity in the forms and kinds of articles sold.
> You could only warrant a certain kind of glazing
> or painting in china, a certain quality of leather or
> cloth, bricks of a certain clay, loaves of a defined
> mixture of meal. Advisable improvements or vari-
> eties in manufacture would have to be examined
> and accepted by the trade guild: when so accepted,
> they would be announced in public reports; and

all puffery and self-proclamation, on the part of tradesmen, absolutely forbidden.

Membership of a guild would be voluntary but Ruskin imagined that non-members would exist in a sort of disreputable *demi-monde*. He saw that some competition from non-guild members was needed as a spur to innovation. But he was unhappy about exposing the public to this dangerous crew:

> Outside of their guild they would have to leave the rogue to puff and cheat as he choose, and the public to be gulled as they chose …
>
> It is always necessary … to leave some safety valve for outlet of irrepressible vice.

These extracts come from *Time and Tide*, a series of letters addressed to Thomas Dixon, a cork-maker from Sunderland. They were published in 1866, as pressure grew to extend the right to vote. Ruskin had no time for democracy. As he aged his authoritarian streak became more pronounced. Having achieved oracular status he began to lay down the law with ever less restraint. *Time and Tide* proposes a corporatist society where people are content with their place. Ruskin does not shy away from the implications, for instance:

> A great deal of the vulgarity, and nearly all the vice, of retail commerce … depends simply on the fact that their minds are always occupied by the vital

(or rather mortal) question of profits. I should at once put an end to this source of baseness by making all retail dealers merely salaried officers in the employ of the trade guilds.

On the plus side, every youngster should be taught a trade and paid enough to start a family. But he should then stay put, with no *feverish hopes* of further betterment. The wealthy should also live more modestly, with fixed limits on their income. All the same, rank and privilege would be baked into the system. There was to be a hierarchy of officials at every level of society:

> over every hundred of the families composing a Christian State, there should be appointed an overseer, or bishop, to render account, to the State, of the life of every individual in those families; and to have care both of their interest and conduct … so that it may be impossible for any person, however humble, to suffer from unknown want, or live in unrecognised crime.

Annual reports on every individual would be sent up the line. There was *nothing un-English* about all this, Ruskin assured Mr Dixon. Nor would there be any nonsense from upstart lawyers. In fact, there would be no lawyers, if by lawyers were meant:

> people who argue about law – not people appointed to administer law … Therefore the youth of this

> landed aristocracy would be trained in my schools,
> to these two great callings … perfect science of
> war, and … perfect science of essential law. And
> from their body shall be chosen the captains and
> judges of England.

In short, the upper echelons would come from the upper classes. Ruskin even suggested paying the nobility – *the noblest monumental architecture of the kingdom* – to live in their castles while giving up their rents. But they were to live frugally. Affluence was to be reserved for the public sphere:

> it is an absolute law of old Communism that
> the fortunes of private persons should be small,
> and of little account in the State; but the com-
> mon treasure of the whole nation should be
> of superb and precious things … as pictures,
> statues, precious books; gold and silver vessels,
> preserved from ancient times; … noble horses,
> cattle, and sheep, on the public lands; and vast
> spaces of land for culture, exercise, and garden,
> round the cities, full of flowers, which, being
> everybody's property, nobody could gather; and
> of birds which, being everybody's property, no-
> body could shoot. And, in a word, that instead
> of a common poverty, or national debt, which
> every poor person in the nation is taxed annually
> to fulfil his part of, there should be a common

wealth, or national reverse of debt, consisting of pleasant things, which every poor person in the nation should be summoned to receive his dole of, annually.

This typical extract comes from *Fors Clavigera*, a collection of letters to the 'Workers and Labourers of Great Britain', whom he liked to address as *we dark-red Communists*. It is a utopian vision, full of far-sighted ideas – public museums, the green belt, national parks, the whole idea that private affluence is unacceptable in the midst of public squalor. But it is also part and parcel of Ruskin's corporatist society, with its medieval guilds. He was surely right that 'wealth' depends on the use we make of it, not just on its quantity. But how do we know what is 'intrinsically' worth having or doing? We still need a way to evaluate options and make decisions. Ruskin rejected the obvious one: a free market, with all its imperfections, humanised and regulated as far as possible through a democratic political process. He struggled to suggest an alternative. The later Ruskin points to the dead end of an essentially static, authoritarian State.

All the same, Ruskin reminds us that markets are there to serve, not command, the society of which they are part and are not the only guide to action. Ruskin was revered in his time as a reformer and champion of the poor. He has influenced progressive thinkers ever since. Ruskin College, Oxford, describes Ruskin (on its website) as a 'radical pioneer of socialist thought'. That he should receive this accolade despite his High Tory leanings suggests the originality of his message and the breadth of its appeal.

During the great pandemic of 2020 some of the worst-paid turned out to be the real 'key workers'. Nurses, bus drivers, cleaners risked and lost their lives to do their duty. They showed, yet again, that most people are not driven by money. As Ruskin had put it in *Unto This Last*:

> In a community regulated only by laws of demand and supply, but protected from open violence, the persons who become rich are, generally speaking, industrious, resolute, proud, covetous, prompt, methodical, sensible, unimaginative, insensitive and ignorant. The persons who remain poor are the entirely foolish, the entirely wise, the idle, the reckless, the humble, the thoughtful, the dull, the imaginative, the sensitive, the well informed, the improvident, the irregularly and impulsively wicked, the clumsy knave, the open thief and the entirely merciful, just and godly person.

WILLIAM MORRIS
1834-1896

Have nothing in your house that you do not know
to be useful, or believe to be beautiful.

THE BEAUTY OF LIFE

These words have made William Morris a hero of the de-cluttering movement. Morris would see clutter as a symptom of a deeper problem, called capitalism. Things, he said, were cheap and nasty because they were made for *profit, not use*. It was his settled belief that that most of our wants are foisted on us by industry and that:

> Civilisation … wastes its own resources, and will
> do so as long as the present system lasts.
> *Useful Work versus Useless Toil,* 1885

Morris himself wasted nothing, least of all his time. He trained as an architect and became a designer, producing fabrics, wallpapers, tapestries and stained glass windows in his own workshops. He founded the Kelmscott Press. He was a poet, author of popular romances and verse epics. He wrote progressive fiction – the

Dream of John Ball and *News from Nowhere* are classics. He moved steadily further left, addressed rallies up and down the country, marched and had himself arrested. His books and poems of protest have inspired idealists ever since.

Morris described his own poetry as *a mere matter of craftsmanship* and said once *if a chap can't compose an epic poem while weaving tapestry, he'd better shut up*. All the same, he was considered an obvious choice to succeed Lord Tennyson as Poet Laureate (which, true to his principles, he refused). He co-founded, funded and helped to write two socialist newspapers but was not too proud – and somehow found the time – to stand on the pavement distributing copies to passers-by. The modesty was deceptive. He was a natural leader who usually ended up in charge. In *How I Became a Socialist* Morris explains how:

> having joined a socialist body, I put some conscience into trying to learn the economical side of socialism, and even tackled Marx, though I must confess that, whereas I thoroughly enjoyed the historical part of *Capital*, I suffered agonies of confusion of the brain over reading the pure economics of that great work.

He was hardly alone in making heavy weather of Marxian economics. He once told a group of socialists that *political economy is not my line and much of it appears to me to be dreary rubbish*. Yet, as a socialist, he was bound to look at things through an economic prism. He spent much of his later life denouncing the economic system and campaigning for a better one.

Economists tend to see work as a cost, if not an unfortunate necessity. To Morris, it was a blessing. In a healthy society, everyone would have fulfilling work that gave them purpose, self-respect and a place in the scheme of things. In capitalist Britain, most people faced a life of pointless drudgery. Such a system was obviously rotten. Work should come with some worthwhile purpose, sufficient time off and a fair reward – all three a distant aspiration for most. Above all it meant:

> The hope of *pleasure* in the work itself: … to all living things there is a pleasure in the exercise of their energies … a man at work, making something which he feels will exist because he is working at it and wills it, is exercising the energies of his mind and soul as well as of his body. Memory and imagination help him as he works. Not only his own thoughts, but the thoughts of the men of past ages guide his hands; and, as a part of the human race, he creates. If we work thus we shall be men, and our days will be happy and eventful. …
>
> All other work but this is worthless; it is slaves' work – mere toiling to live, that we may live to toil.

Capitalism led to *slaves' work*. Instead of everyone doing their fair share, most work was forced on the poor, who

> work so hard that they may be said to do nothing else … and are accordingly called 'the working classes'.

Morris was not exaggerating. When he wrote this in 1888, a typical working week was around 70 hours – for the lucky ones with a full time job. Dock workers were hired by the day or even the hour – men fought each other for scraps of work. Morris thought most work was wasted. Domestic service was an obvious example. Commercial competition used up an army of clerks and salesmen in a pointless war for market share. Whatever labour was left for making things went mostly into luxuries for the rich. For the poor there was only time to make shoddy, adulterated stuff – another form of waste:

> [The workers] must put up … with coarse food that does not nourish, with rotten raiment which does not shelter, with wretched houses. .. [and] even lend a hand to the great industrial invention of the age – adulteration, and by its help produce for their own use shams and mockeries of the luxury of the rich …
>
> This cheapness is necessary to the system of exploiting on which modern manufacture rests. In other words, our society includes a great mass

of slaves, who must be fed, clothed, housed and amused as slaves, and that their daily necessity compels them to make the slave-wares whose use is the perpetuation of their slavery.

Useful Work versus Useless Toil

Waste was a product of gross inequality, compounded by the market system. Because things were made for profit not for use, they were 'adulterated', like margarine (a pet hate, often cited by Morris to show the horrors of capitalism). Competition led to commercial slumps (the 1880s saw a worldwide slowdown, with falling prices, profits and wages in many sectors). There was a constant race to the bottom, led by 'gamblers' wanting to make things more cheaply:

competition 'stimulates production' … indeed it does do that; but what kind of production? Well, production of something to sell at a profit, or say production of profits…

Well you may say, but it cheapens the goods. In a sense it does; and yet only apparently, as wages have a tendency to sink for the ordinary worker in proportion as prices sink; and at what a cost do we gain this appearance of cheapness! Plainly speaking, at the cost of cheating the consumer and starving the real producer for the benefit of the gambler…

Taking him in the lump, the consumer is

perfectly helpless against the gambler; the goods
are forced on him by their cheapness, and with
them a certain kind of life which that ... aggressive
cheapness determines for him.

How We Live and How We Might Live, 1887

To keep down costs, industry had to keep expand-
ing in a vicious circle of cheapness and exploitation. As
a craftsman, Morris admired pre-industrial societies. He
watched with horror as they vanished into the maw of
global capitalism:

the traditions of a thousand years fall before it in
a month; it overruns a weak or semi-barbarous
country, and whatever romance or pleasure or art
existed there, is trodden down into a mire of sor-
didness and ugliness; the Indian or Javanese crafts-
man may no longer ply his craft leisurely, working
a few hours a day, in producing a maze of strange
beauty on a piece of cloth: a steam-engine is set
a-going at Manchester ... and the Asiatic worker,
if he is not starved to death outright, as plenti-
fully happens, is driven himself into a factory to
lower the wages of his Manchester brother worker
... The South Sea Islander must leave his canoe--
carving, his sweet rest, and his graceful dances, and
become the slave of a slave: trousers, shoddy, rum,
missionary, and fatal disease.

Morris had no time for 'Demand and Supply'. The Demand side was distorted by the needs of an unequal society. The Supply side was a form of gambling driven by the search for profit, leading to periodic slumps which caused appalling misery. There was nothing 'free' about the system:

> because the privileged classes have at their back the force of the Executive by means of which to compel the unprivileged to accept the terms; if this is 'free competition' there is no meaning in words.

The opposite of all this was cooperation. Morris thought socialism would make a much better job of producing what people really needed:

> what Socialism offers you … is, once more, regulation of the markets; supply and demand commensurate; no gambling, and consequently … no waste; not overwork and weariness for the worker one month, and the next no work and terror of starvation, but steady work and plenty of leisure every month; not cheap market wares, that is to say, adulterated wares, with scarcely any good in them, mere scaffold-poles for building up profits … Not these, but such goods as best fulfilled the real uses of the consumers would labour be set to make; for, profit being abolished, people could have what they wanted instead of what the profit-grinders at home and abroad forced them to take.

There would be health for all, education for all, and worthwhile work for all. The rough work would be shared, if it must be done at all. Morris had worked alongside his men in the heat and smell of the dying sheds. He assumed that everyone would do their fair share:

> I should think very little of ... a stout and healthy man who did not feel a pleasure in doing rough work; always supposing ... that it was useful (and consequently honoured), and that it was not continuous or hopeless, and that he was really doing it of his own free will.

Socialism would bring in a virtuous circle. As workers tasted the fruits of their own effort, so they would enjoy their work and need no other incentive. They would find that:

> after a little, people would rather be anxious to seek work than to avoid it; that our working hours would rather be merry parties of men and maids, young men and old enjoying themselves over their work, than the grumpy weariness it mostly is now. Then would come the time for the new birth of art, so much talked of, so long deferred; people could not help showing their mirth and pleasure in their work ... and the workshop would once more be a school of art.

Though a communist with anarchic leanings, Morris looked back to the Middle Ages for inspiration. He did so as a keen historian. In the *Aims of Art* (1887) he weighed the pros and cons of medieval life:

> I quite admit that the oppression and violence of the Middle Ages had its effect on the art of those days, its shortcomings are traceable to them; they repressed art in certain directions, I do not doubt that … But I do say that it was possible then to have social, organic, hopeful progressive art …
>
> The mediaeval craftsman was free in his work, therefore he made it as amusing to himself as he could; and it was his pleasure and not his pain that made all things beautiful that were made, and lavished treasures of human hope and thought on everything that man made, from a cathedral to a porridge-pot. Come, let us put it in the way least respectful to the mediaeval craftsman, most polite to the modern 'hand': the poor devil of the fourteenth century, his work was of so little value that he was allowed to waste it by the hour in pleasing himself – and others.

The ideal would be a cooperative system, on the lines of medieval guilds. In *Art and Industry in the Fourteenth Century* (1889) Morris explained how guild rules governed pay, hours of work, apprenticeship, quality, ingredients and so forth. It was all designed to spread the work around, ensure the quality of the product, and prevent any one man from dominating the trade:

Now you will see that the accumulation of capital is impossible under such regulations as these, and it was meant to be impossible. The theory of industry among these communes was something like this. There is a certain demand for the goods which we can make, and a certain settled population to make them: if the goods are not thoroughly satisfactory we shall lose our market for them and be ruined: we must therefore keep up their quality to the utmost. Furthermore, the work to be done must be shared amongst the whole of those who can do it, who must be sure of work always as long as they are well behaved and industrious, and also must have a fair livelihood and plenty of leisure; as why should they not?

As a young man Morris visited Rouen Cathedral. It became his standard of perfection. His imagination fed off the Middle Ages – but a rather selective one. In *News from Nowhere,* he imagined waking up sometime after 2003 in his beloved Hammersmith.* The city has given way to a rural idyll. The Thames flows pure and teems with salmon. People wear homespun clothes of vaguely medieval design. They call each other 'neighbour' and help each other at every turn. They seem relaxed and friendly.

It turns out that Communism came to England after a short and fairly painless revolution in the 1950s. There

* Where his home, Kelmscott House, is now a museum.

were teething troubles, of course. But William Guest (the time-travelling narrator) finds himself in a London that has shrunk back to its medieval self, a collection of pleasant villages surrounding a small urban core. It is a self-governing community, more anarchist than communist, medieval in appearance – save that there is no king, aristocracy, or church. There is no crime and there are no prisons. Everyone is educated but there are no schools. For women, it is the Middle Ages without nunneries or ducking stools: they lead an independent life and make the most of it (William is captivated). Above all, there is no money and yet everyone has what they need.

This splendid economy works through a spontaneous communal effort. People enjoy taking a turn at different tasks. William needs to cross the Thames. Dick, the ferryman, rows him across but takes no payment since money no longer exists. If Dick really needs something from a shop he simply asks for it. Even international trade seems to work on this principle – William is given French claret in the communal guesthouse and Turkish tobacco in the tobacconist's. Dick's friend, a bookish weaver, needs some outdoor work for a change. He takes over the ferry for a few days while Dick takes William to see his great-grandfather. 'Old Hammond' is a historian who explains the system and its origins. William asks:

> 'How do you get people to work when there is no reward of labour, and especially how do you get them to work strenuously?'

'But no reward of labour?' said Hammond, gravely. 'The reward of labour is life. Is that not enough?'

'But no reward for especially good work,' quoth I.

'Plenty of reward,' said he – 'the reward of creation. The wages which God gets, as people might have said time agone. If you are going to be paid for the pleasure of creation, which is what excellence in work means, the next thing we shall hear of will be a bill sent in for the begetting of children.

What, asks William, about the *natural desire not to work*? Hammond tells him the idea is meaningless:

because it implies that all work is suffering, and we are so far from thinking that, that, as you may have noticed, there is a kind of fear growing up among us that we shall one day be short of work. It is a pleasure we are afraid of losing, not a pain.

Hammond describes the old order, when health, happiness, and leisure were sacrificed to 'cheap production':

a most elaborate system of buying and selling, which has been called the World Market; and that World Market, once set a-going, forced them to go on making more and more of these wares, whether they needed them or not. So that while (of course) they could not free themselves from the toil of making real necessaries, they created in a never-ending series, sham, or artificial necessaries, which became, under the iron rule of the aforesaid World-Market, of equal importance to them with the real necessaries which supported life. By all this they burdened themselves with a prodigious amount of work, merely for the sake of keeping their wretched system going.

Morris saw that growth had to stop one day. So did leading economists. Ricardo foresaw a stagnant economy as competition snuffed out opportunities for profit. J. S. Mill and Keynes looked forward to a time of material plenty, when people would abandon growth to pursue the higher things of life. Adam Smith expected the economy to end up in a 'stationary state' but was worried about this. Growth was the 'cheerful and hearty' state; a stagnant society was a miserable place, especially for the poor. Morris imagined a stationary economy that provided work for all, met all legitimate needs, yet preserved the social fabric and the environment. However, this static economy came with a static society, providing no room to evolve or tackle problems. The Houses of Parliament had become *a storage place for manure.* Old Hammond tells Will *we are well off as to politics because we have none.* This reflects Morris's own beliefs. He rejected the parliamentary route to socialism, seeing Parliament as a tool in the hands of the rich. He really thought that political problems would melt away in a communist society. With no class conflicts to settle, any residual problems would be solved locally, by majority vote:

> in the assemblies of a Communal Society, there would be no opposition of interests, but only divergencies of opinion, as to the best way of doing what all were agreed to do. So that the minority would give way without any feeling of injury.
>
> *Why I am a Communist*, 1894

Morris managed to run a successful business and lead a political splinter-group while remaining a complete innocent at heart. He was patronised, sponged-off and cheated by his entourage but retained a saint-like faith in human nature. As Michel Houellebecq puts it:

> the model of society proposed by William Morris would not be utopian at all in a world where everyone resembled William Morris.*

As a political thinker Morris points to a dead end. As a craftsman he has much to say to a world drowning in waste: consume wisely, prefer the organic, the lasting, the

---

* Houellebecq introduces himself as a character in his novel *The Map and the Territory* and puts these words into his own mouth. They round off a discussion of Morris, whose influence on later generations plays a part in the plot. One of the other characters in the novel is a lecturer in economics who has fallen out with the subject and suspects that the theories she teaches are 'pure and simple charlatanism'.

handmade, reject what is ugly, wasteful or polluting. As he constantly pointed out, wise consumption and a fair society promote each other. He would not be surprised to find that fast fashion is an appalling polluter and relies on exploiting cheap labour in the sweat-shops of Asia. It is the epitome of all he disliked. His words on work should also resonate in a world where precarious, soul-destroying jobs are still the lot of many:

> the pleasurable exercise of our energies is the end
> of life and the cause of happiness.
>
> *Arts and Crafts of Today,* 1889

An economy based on this principle would look rather different. Morris would tell us to make space for small scale, craft-based workers of every sort. He would tell us to recycle and repair, not chuck and replace. He would surely hate to see the arts of life turned into commodities. He would urge us to make space, beyond the reach of the market, for a more sustainable, homespun way of life. Morris thought capitalism would choke on its own waste. Instead, it was communism that died while capitalism has continued on its way, helped by a new industry of de-cluttering consultants. He might be surprised and disappointed, but he seemed aware that communism might not go to plan:

> I pondered all these things, and how men fight
> and lose the battle, and the thing that they fought
> for comes about in spite of their defeat, and when

it comes turns out not to be what they meant, and other men have to fight for what they meant under another name.

A Dream of John Ball, 1887

GEORGE BERNARD SHAW
1856-1950

Mendoza: *I am a brigand: I live by robbing the rich.*
Tanner: *I am a gentleman: I live by robbing the poor.*
Shake hands.

MAN AND SUPERMAN, ACT III

In 1924 Bernard Shaw's sister in law asked for a short
introduction to socialism, suitable for her discussion
group. Three years later she received a 200,000 word
book, *The Intelligent Woman's Guide to Socialism and Cap-
italism.* In the interval Shaw won the Nobel Prize for Lit-
erature. The citation praised his work for 'idealism and
humanity, its stimulating satire often being infused with a
singular poetic beauty.' *The Intelligent Woman's Guide* was
published in 1928 and received with all the deference due
to a world famous sage. It was 'the world's most impor-
tant book since the Bible', said Ramsey MacDonald who
became Prime Minister a year later.*

---

* Which suggests that 'intelligent men' read the book too. There were
some comments, even then, about the condescending title and tone of
the book. Shaw supported women's rights, e.g. to the vote. In his plays
women come across as much the stronger sex. But he was never one for
political correctness.

Shaw began as a penniless Irish writer, struggling for a toehold in London. Like Karl Marx he studied economics in the Reading Room at the British Museum. For the next seventy years these researches would inform a torrent of articles, pamphlets and plays on economic issues. Shaw was not a modest man: he once spent two hours explaining socialism to Stalin. He preached his brand of economics with complete self-assurance:

> You will find quite a number of professional economists who know nothing of political economy and never will. They are attracted to it by their natural incapacity for it, just as, on the stage, the man who is naturally a comedian craves the tragedian's part…
>
> The economists of the future will have to be philosophers dealing with human conduct and destiny in the largest sense, international as well as national. The field of the political economist will be life; and his instrument will be literature.
>
> *Life, Literature and Political Economy,* 1905

In other words economics needed a man to give the subject purpose: someone like Bernard Shaw. Most economists were hirelings, paid to explain away poverty – *the greatest of our evils and the worst of our crimes:*

> we tolerate poverty as if it were either a wholesome tonic for lazy people or else a virtue to be embraced as St Francis embraced it…

Now what does this 'Let Him Be Poor mean'? It means let him be weak. Let him be ignorant. Let him become a nucleus of disease. Let him be a standing exhibition and example of ugliness and dirt. Let him have rickety children. Let him be cheap and let him drag his fellows down to his price by selling himself to do their work. Let his habitations turn our cities into poisonous congeries of slums. Let his daughters infect our young men with the diseases of the streets...

We allow our industry to be organised in open reliance on the maintenance of a 'reserve army of the unemployed' for the sake of 'elasticity'...

It is for the poor to repudiate poverty when they have had enough of it. The thing can be done easily enough: the demonstrations to the contrary by economists ... hired by the rich to defend them, or even doing the work gratuitously out of sheer folly and abjectness, impose only on those who want to be imposed on.

Preface to *Major Barbara*, 1907

Shaw began as a 'Fabian' socialist, a believer in reform not revolution. In 1884 he set out the Fabian creed in fourteen points.* These three give the flavour:

* Second Fabian Pamphlet. The Fabians are named after a Roman general, famous for achieving victory by putting off the decisive action until victory was certain.

That, under existing circumstances, wealth cannot be enjoyed without dishonour, or foregone without misery.

That the most striking result of our present system of farming out the national Land and Capital to private individuals has been the division of Society into hostile classes, with large appetites and no dinners at one extreme, and large dinners and no appetites at the other.

That the practice of entrusting the Land of the nation to private persons in the hope that they will make the best of it has been discredited by the consistency with which they have made the worst of it; and that the Nationalisation of the Land in some form is a public duty.

These ideas gained fuller form in the *Fabian Essays* of 1889, a best-seller to which Shaw contributed *The Economic Basis of Socialism*, and *The Transition* (an historical survey). In essence, Shaw set out to replace Marxian economics with a Fabian alternative. Marx was magnificent but misguided, his labour theory of value a mystical irrelevance, his proletarian revolution destructive and unnecessary. As Shaw pointed out in *The Perfect Wagnerite* (1898):

I know ten times as much of economics and a hundred times as much of practical administration as Marx did.

There was a much better road to socialism. It began
with Ricardo's theory of rent. This showed how economic
growth gradually creates a property-owning class, able to
live off unearned income ('rent'); and how these wind-
fall gains consume an ever-growing share of the cake. The
implication was obvious: nationalise land, confiscate or
tax away all unearned incomes, and the road to socialism
lay open. As well as landowners there was now an army
of urban 'rentiers', living off dividends and interest pay-
ments. Shaw had no time for such drones. Economists
used to describe dividends as the reward of 'superior skill'
and interest payments as the 'reward of abstinence'. Shaw
could never ignore a red rag: these were value judgements
dressed up as science:

> The notion that the people who are now spending
> in week-end hotels, in motor cars, in Switzerland,
> the Riviera, and Algeria … have ever invented an-
> ything, ever directed anything, ever even selected
> their own investments without the aid of a stock-
> broker or solicitor, ever as much as seen the indus-
> tries from which their incomes are derived, betrays
> not only the most rustic ignorance of economic
> theory, but a practical ignorance of society so in-
> credible...
>
> *Socialism and Superior Brains* 1910

Capital was 'spare money', amassed by the rich in pre-
vious rounds of exploitation:

> In this way capital can claim to be the result of
> saving, or, as one ingenious apologist neatly put
> it, the reward of abstinence, a gleam of humour
> which still enlivens treatises on capital. The savers,
> it need hardly be said, are those who have more
> money than they want to spend: the abstainers are
> those who have less.
>
> *Economic Basis of Socialism* 1889

Economists claimed that prices were set at the 'margin', where rents dwindled to zero; consequently, they had no effect on prices. To Shaw this was pure sophistry.* Most production took place inside the 'margin', giving rise to huge windfall gains for the rentiers. These came out of the poor man's necessities. It was:

> a trick by which the ordinary economist tries to
> cheat us into accepting the private property system
> as practically just … This trivially ingenious way of
> being disingenuous is officially taught as political
> economy in our schools to this day. … it is mere
> thimblerig.

The essence of capitalism was that money went to money. The community worked together to produce the physical and intellectual capital, from railways to scientific discoveries, on which civilisation depended. But in the end, it all belonged to the capitalist:

---

* See pp. 118-20 for De Quincey's struggle with the problem of rent.

If a railway is required, all that is necessary is to provide subsistence for a sufficient number of labourers to construct it. If, for example, the railway requires the labour of a thousand men for five years, the cost to the proprietors of the site is the subsistence of a thousand men for five years. This subsistence is technically called capital. It is provided by the proprietors … At the end of the five years, the completed railway is the property of the capitalists; and the railway makers fall back into the labour market as helpless as they were before.

Growing inequality led to an ever grosser misallocation of resources. Ruskin's 'illth' was endemic. Riches increased (private affluence) even as wealth declined (public squalor). In a highly unequal society private utility was a hopeless guide to value:

wealth is steadily decreasing with the spread of poverty. But riches are increasing, which is quite another thing … the accumulation of riches, and consequently of an excessive purchasing power, in the hands of a class, soon satiates that class with socially useful wealth, and sets them offering a price for luxuries … A New York lady, for instance, having a nature of exquisite sensibility, orders an elegant rosewood and silver coffin, upholstered in pink satin, for her dead dog. It is made; and meanwhile a live child is prowling barefooted and hunger-stunted in the frozen gutter outside. The exchange-value of the coffin is counted as part of the national wealth; but a nation which cannot afford food and clothing for its children cannot be allowed to pass as wealthy because it has provided a pretty coffin for a dead dog. Exchange value itself, in fact, has become bedevilled like everything else, and represents, no longer utility, but the cravings of lust, folly, vanity, gluttony, and madness, technically described by genteel economists as 'effective demand.'

In short, capitalism was too intolerable to survive:

This, then, is the economic analysis which convicts Private Property of being unjust even from the beginning, … All attempts yet made to construct true societies upon it have failed: the nearest things to societies so achieved have been civilisations, which have rotted into centres of vice and luxury, and eventually been swept away by uncivilised races. That our own civilisation is already in an advanced stage of rottenness may be taken as statistically proved.

Income tax had established the principle of taking back from the rich what they had taken from the poor. All forms of income from private property should be redistributed since they were:

paid out of the difference between the produce of the worker's labour and the price of that labour sold in the open market for wages, salary, fees, or profits. The whole, except economic rent, can be added directly to the incomes of the workers by simply discontinuing its exaction from them. Economic rent, arising as it does from variations of fertility or advantages of situation, must always be held as common or social wealth, and used … for public purposes, among which Socialism would make national insurance and the provision of capital matters of the first importance.

This was Shaw's 'Fabian' route to socialism. It would come to pass not through violence but by the force of reason, as marshalled by Fabians like himself:

The science of the production and distribution of wealth is Political Economy. Socialism appeals to that science, and, turning on Individualism its own guns, routs it in incurable disaster…

While waiting for this to happen Shaw spent six years as a Councillor for St Pancras. The district had some of the poorest, most insanitary streets in London. It was the perfect test bed for his ideas, for instance that the city should make its own electricity and gas and build its own houses. His ideas were listened to politely but ignored. Vested interests and innate conservatism saw to that. Eventually Shaw gave up local government in disgust but he drew on the experience for years to come. It also led to a pamphlet on *The Common Sense of Municipal Trading* (1904), arguing that public services were better and cheaper than private ones, which only seemed more efficient because most of their true costs were borne by the public sector:

> suppose the drink trade were debited with what it costs in disablement, inefficiency, illness and crime, with all their depressing effects on industrial productivity, and with their direct costs in doctors, policemen, prisons etc! Suppose at the same time that the municipal bridges and highways account were credited with the value of the time and wear and tear saved by them!
>
> Commercial contractors have no responsibility for their men, beyond paying them. The Council is responsible for them 'from the cradle to the grave'. Consequently private companies can and do make large profits out of sweated and demoralised labour at the expense of the ratepayers; and these very profits are often cited as proofs of the superior efficiency of private enterprise.

Shaw had mixed views on monetary matters, perhaps reflecting his position as a socialist with a rich wife and (by the 1920s) a large income from his plays. He had no faith in a paper currency because of his general contempt for the political class. This put him in the odd position of supporting the gold standard, the totem of high-Tory bankers:

> the most sacred economic duty of a Government is to keep the value of money steady…
>
> You have to choose (as a voter) between trusting to the natural stability of gold and the … honesty and intelligence of the members of the Government. And, with due respect for these gentlemen, I advise you, as long as the Capitalist system lasts, to vote for gold.

But banking was far too important to leave to private bankers. Making loans was a lucrative business made possible by a sound currency – which was provided by the community. It was a natural State monopoly and should be nationalised:

> No wonder the bankers, who make enormous profits, and consequently have the greatest dread of having these cut off by the nationalisation of banking, declare that no Government could possibly do this difficult work of hiring out money, and that it must be left to them, as they alone understand it! Now, to begin with, they neither understand it nor do it themselves. Their bad advice produced widespread ruin in Europe after the war.

Banking staff should be scrupulous with other people's money, neither too bold nor too cautious in the loans they made. In short, they should be like civil servants, so they might as well work for the Government. However, interest rates were themselves an anomaly, caused by inequality. Capital was 'spare money', a luxury confined to a tiny minority. He foresaw the day when capital would be abundant and interest rates negative (a vision now coming true):

> a woman who found herself with a tenpenny loaf on her hands over and above what her family needed to eat, might, sooner than throw the loaf into the dustbin, say to her neighbour, 'You can have this loaf if you will give me half a fresh loaf for it next week': that is to say, she might offer half the loaf for the service of saving her from the total loss of it by natural decay.
>
> The economists call this paying negative interest. What it means is that you pay people to keep your Spare money for you until you want it instead of making them pay you for allowing them to keep it, which the economists call paying positive interest.
>
> One is just as natural as the other; and the sole reason why nobody at present will pay you to borrow from them, whereas everyone will pay you to lend to them, is that under our system of unequal division of income there are so very few of us with spare money to lend, and so very many with less than they need ... If instead of having a

few rich amid a great many poor, we had a great
many rich, the bankers would charge you a high
price for keeping your money.

These extracts on banking come from the *The Intelligent Woman's Guide to Socialism and Capitalism* (if nothing else, the *Guide* was a monument to mansplaining).
For most social ills the *Guide* prescribed the same cure:
an equal distribution of income. Late in life Shaw began
to wonder how it would work in practice. He tackled the
problem in *How Much Money Do We Need?*. On a visit to
Soviet Russia he was told that *to maintain an intellectual
proletariat … it is necessary to distribute income in wages
and salaries at rates varying as widely as ten to one*. An equal
share for everyone was the ideal but Shaw calculated that
it would leave only a few shillings a week to live on. For
that money you would never find doctors or scientists. :

> Equality of income must begin with a basic in-
> come large enough to produce Prime Ministers,
> higher mathematicians, historians and philoso-
> phers, authors and artists as well as ploughmen
> and dairymaids.

Shaw thought £800 p.a. would do the trick. The most
important jobs could be capped at this level while eco-
nomic growth allowed the rest to catch up. A subsistence
wage was then around £100 p.a., and the average less
than £300 p.a. Shaw's £800 would be around £80,000 in
today's money. He was onto something: recent research

suggests that beyond this level extra earnings bring little extra happiness.* But Shaw had a wider aim: to improve the human race, of which he had a dim view:

> The majority of men at present in Europe have no business to be alive; and no serious progress will be made until we address ourselves earnestly and scientifically to the task of producing trustworthy human material for society. In short, it is necessary to breed a race of men in whom the life giving impulses predominate…
>
> *The Perfect Wagnerite* 1897

Unearned income produced effete young men, rich enough to marry one of Shaw's heroines but without the 'life force' to win her, let alone breed the man of the future. Shaw's plays are full of them. Egalitarianism was a biological as well as a political necessity: to eliminate the chinless wonder, cut off his income and leave the field to a new type of 'superman', able to father some decent human beings. *How Much Money Do We Need?* appeared in 1944, the same year as the Beveridge Report which laid out a blueprint for the Welfare State. But Shaw was now thinking on a different plane:

> What is to be the test of sufficient equality to make a civilisation stable and secure? … The test will be

---

* In 2010, a famous study by Angus Deaton and Daniel Kahneman of Princeton University put the figure at $75,000.

inter-marriageability. When the astronomer's son can marry the housemaid without the slightest misalliance, the trick will be done as far as law or policy can or need do it.

Shaw was far too busy to have children himself but otherwise full of 'life force'. By the end of his career he had made a fortune. He allowed himself a Rolls Royce and a chauffeur but preferred to drive himself, which he did with gusto. There were accidents and many close shaves. His passengers must have smiled when he compared capitalism to a 'runaway car':

> CAPITALISM, then, keeps us in perpetual motion. Now motion is not a bad thing … Changeable women, for instance, are more endurable than monotonous ones …
>
> Motion is delightful when we can control it, guide it, and stop it when it is taking us into danger … Uncontrolled motion is terrible … Capital is running away with us; and we know that it has always ended in the past by taking its passengers over the brink of the precipice at the foot of which are strewn the ruins of empires.
>
> *Intelligent Woman's Guide*

Shaw's views darkened with the general outlook. He never had much respect for democracy. When the franchise was extended (in 1918) to all working men and to women over thirty, the result was a massacre for the

Labour party. His cult of the superman grew out of despair:

> after all, the dog will return to his vomit … we may as well make up our minds that Man will return to his idols and his cupidities, in spite of all 'movements' and revolutions, until his nature is changed … Until then, his early success in building commercial civilisations … are but preliminaries to the inevitable later stage, now threatening us, in which the passions which built the civilisation become fatal instead of productive.

Democracy was still the safest option: Shaw advised the 'intelligent woman' to *stick to your vote as hard as you can*. But contempt for capitalism blinded him to the evils of other systems. In 1937 he published a new edition of the *Guide*, expanded to cover Soviet communism and fascism. He expected fascism to end in disaster but only because it was hand in glove with capitalism:

> the average citizen is fascist by nature and education …
>
> So far fascism is better than Liberalism … in so far as it produces a United Front with a public outlook; but as long as it maintains private property it must … end in a social morass of general poverty and exceptional riches, slavery and parasitism.

Meanwhile he was absurdly indulgent towards Soviet communism. Writing shortly after Stalin's show trials and the mass starvation of the Ukraine, he offered such insights as:

> Fortunately mistakes are not hushed up in Russia: they are attacked and embedded with uncompromising vigour.

> At present there is not a hungry child in the fully Sovietised regions of Russia.

When Shaw taught himself economics Queen Victoria was still on the throne. Theories devised for a vanished era were no guide to a world faced with Hitler and Stalin. Shaw was a prisoner of obsolete economics, as Maynard Keynes explained in 1934:

> That system bred two families – those who thought it true and inevitable, and those who thought it true and intolerable. There was no third school of thought in the nineteenth century. Nevertheless, there is a third possibility – that it is not true; and this will allow us to escape without revolution or socialism.*

Shaw lived to see a Labour government set up the

* Article in the *New Statesman* (November 1934), cited in Robert Skidelsky's life of Keynes, vol. 2 *The Economist as Saviour,* pp. 518-521, along with a wonderful exchange of letters between Keynes and Shaw.

Welfare State and the NHS. It was not his idea of socialism: the capitalists were still in charge, the unions now complicit in the system. By this stage he was used to being admired but ignored. His real legacy to economics is the London School of Economics, of which he was a co-founder (his wife Charlotte was also an active and generous benefactor). It is a typical Shaw paradox. The LSE exists to apply reason to economic and social affairs. If that requires a belief in 'rational economic man', Shaw never got the message:

> Life is a thing of which it is important to have a theory; yet most people take it for granted and go on living for no better reason than that they find themselves alive … We are here wearing absurd costumes and in many ways behaving ourselves like lunatics. Clearly the force behind us is neither reasonable in our sense of the word, nor concerned with our individual ease and happiness …
>
> Man, the supreme organism, is an extremely dangerous and ugly animal. Aristophanes and Swift represent him, quite rationally, as being physically despised by birds and morally loathed by horses. He is not even wise in his own individual affairs; for no man manages his affairs as well as a tree does.

HILAIRE BELLOC
1870-1953

When I am dead, I hope it may be said
His sins were scarlet but his books were read.

ON HIS BOOKS

Hilaire Belloc spent like a Lord, was often short of money and wrote too many potboilers. But occasionally he struck gold. Even those who never read verse might have come across *Cautionary Tales for Children*, which appeared in 1907:

> Matilda told such Dreadful Lies,
> It made one gasp and stretch ones eyes…

The *Tales* describe a vanished world yet have an ageless appeal. Belloc's genius with light verse rested on a lifelong habit of writing poetry. Much of it came from the heart: poems about his beloved Sussex Downs, his friends, his Catholic faith. He was born in 1870 to a French father and English mother, on the eve of the Franco-Prussian war. The family home on the outskirts of Paris was ransacked by Prussian soldiers. Two years later Belloc's father died and the family moved back to London. Here, as

Catholics, they found themselves part of a rather beleaguered minority. Belloc soon took the fight to the enemy. He appointed himself defender of the faith, a role he performed with gusto for the rest of his life.

If France was Belloc's first love, England was the lasting one. After national service, as a French artilleryman, he went up to Oxford. Here he found an Elysian field, won every prize, became a part of undergraduate myth and wrote one of the great celebrations of the Oxford idyll, his much quoted *Dedicatory Ode*:

> From quiet homes and first beginning,
> Out to the undiscovered ends,
> There's nothing worth the wear of winning,
> But laughter and the love of friends.

There followed a happy marriage, children, early promise as a writer, pundit and politician. There were setbacks too. Rejection by All Souls College ended the love affair with Oxford. A spell as a Liberal MP (1906-10) ended in failure and bitterness, giving Belloc a lifelong disdain for Parliament. His mother fell for a rogue financier who lost her fortune on the stock market. His wife died in her prime, on the eve of the First Wold War. As the war drew to a close, his eldest son was killed in action. Though adored by his friends, he became a rather isolated figure, an outsider, always rowing against the tide.

Belloc's most lasting prose work is an account of a pilgrimage. *The Path to Rome* (1902) begins in Toul, scene of his soldiering days on the Franco-German border. It takes him, on foot, over the Alps and the Apennines. En route, the book becomes a tour of Belloc's mind. It was his habit to attend Mass every day. This gave him a feeling of communion with the culture and history of Europe, a feeling *that that you are doing what the human race has done for thousands upon thousands of years*. In the Swiss village of Undervellier he found the whole population at evening Mass, intoning the familiar prayers. Mass in those days was said in Latin, making it universal across space and time:

> My whole mind was taken up and transfigured
> by this collective act, and I saw for a moment the
> Catholic Church quite plain, and I remembered
> Europe and the centuries.

Along the way Belloc met an anarchist who wished there were no property, no armies and no governments. He replied that strong roots, a country to love and a just cause to fight for are among the great blessings of life:

> and as for property, a man on his own land was the
> nearest to God.

This was the outlook that Belloc brought to bear on economics. Though self-taught in the subject he had guidance from a higher source. In 1891 Pope Leo XIII issued *Rerum Novarum*, a new doctrine on social and economic policy. As a Papal Encyclical it was binding on the whole

Church. It shaped Belloc's economic thinking from then on. In essence, the Pope condemned both the injustices of capitalism and the 'false promises' of socialism. Class conflict was not inevitable. Human beings aspired to own property and pass it on to their children: this was a fundamental fact. Crass materialism, exploitation and injustice were another matter. Contracts, including wage bargains, were not legitimate when based on the abuse of power. The rich could look after themselves: the State had a duty to protect the poor, who also had a right (within limits) to organise in defence of their own interests. In the ideal society, property ownership would be widely spread and justice would be 'distributive':

> The law, therefore, should favour ownership, and its policy should be to induce as many as possible of the people to become owners...
>
> Men always work harder and more readily when they work on that which belongs to them; nay, they learn to love the very soil that yields in response to the labour of their hands, not only food to eat, but an abundance of good things for themselves and those that are dear to them.
>
> *Rerum Novarum*

The 'Distributist' movement came into being to propagate these ideas, with Belloc (and G. K. Chesterton) to the fore. Distributism has been much lampooned as offering 'three acres and a cow'. Traditional communities of peasant farmers were indeed Belloc's ideal; he would cite parts of Denmark, Ireland or rural France as nearest to a Distributive society. He did not expect to see such a society in Britain but was horrified by the alternative. The industrial world was drifting towards a *Servile State*, the title of his best known work on political economy.

Belloc put power at the centre of economics. He insisted that big business was as much of a threat to free markets as government. He would have ridiculed the idea that all power is surrendered to the impersonal play of the market;* and insisted that imbalances in power shape transactions just as much as 'utility' or cost. Belloc rejected capitalism because it put ownership of the means of production in a few hands, leaving the vast majority as wage-slaves. Such a society could never be truly free because *Freedom involves property*. A socialist society would be even worse. It would still need capital, which would still be controlled by a tiny elite. Because socialism went against the grain of human nature it had never been put into practice (this was 1912).

The alternative was a 'Distributive State' in which most people owned the means to earn a livelihood – a farm, a workshop, an inn or a store. In principle, a

---

* A belief also ridiculed by the great American economist J. K. Galbraith: 'Nothing is so important in the defence of the modern corporation as the argument that power does not exist; that all power is surrendered to the impersonal play of the market. Nothing is more serviceable than the resultant conditioning of the young to that belief.' *The Anatomy of Power*

Distributive State seemed to Belloc entirely realistic, since this model had existed in most societies for most of history. In Britain, however, it was probably past restoring, after centuries of drift in the wrong direction. All had been well in the Middle Ages. For most practical purposes the peasants' land was their own. Trade and industry were controlled by guilds, which kept up standards while ensuring a reasonable living to all their members. The rot set in when Henry VIII dissolved the monasteries and distributed their land among his favourites, creating a class with vast disposable wealth. In due course, this pool of capital called forth a financial system to match. Capitalism was born: a disruptive force that would end the old order, empty the villages and drive a dispossessed horde into the mill towns and poorhouses of industrial England. As Belloc put it:

> The industrial revolution took the form it did because of pre-existing inequalities which it magnified to an intolerable degree.

Without proper safeguards, a healthy dispersion of wealth was never secure. Capitalism worked by concentrating wealth in ever fewer hands. It was inherently destabilising. and could not last. The gap between moral theory and social fact was too great. Above all: *capitalism destroys security*. Most people were resigned to wage-slavery and lived in chronic fear of the sack. A degree of security and comfort was all they asked for. It would all end with an unholy alliance between capitalism and the State, to deliver just such a '*Servile State*':

> Capitalism must keep alive, by non-Capitalist methods, great masses of the population who would otherwise starve to death.

There was plenty of room in Belloc's vast oeuvre for a text book. *Economics for Helen* appeared in 1924. It was addressed to the teenage daughter of a much loved friend. She must have found it hard going. Belloc tries to be simple but soon veers into metaphysics:

> It is not the horse itself which constitutes ... wealth, but something attaching to the horse… it is this value which is wealth… It is… the ability to get other wealth in exchange which constitutes true economic wealth.

Economics for Helen amounted to a re-hash of *The Servile State* plus some economic theory and a long section on finance. Belloc explained how banks worked and why they played such a critical part in a modern economy. In the early days banks had met a real need but had since become a menace. As the distributors of credit, they had the power to make or break a business. They held vast amounts of information about the rest of the community. Worst of all, in a paper currency system they could create credit out of thin air. Such power could only lead to abuse. A revolt was brewing:

> There will inevitably be a struggle between the
> banking, or financial, interests and the people all
> over civilised countries: but no one can tell which
> will win. In industrial countries, the odds are in
> favour of the banks, or financiers.

Three years later Belloc got his way over paper money. Britain returned to the gold standard, a disastrous experiment that was soon abandoned. In other ways his warnings sound prescient. He suggested that small, co-operatively owned banks, linked to their regions or trades, should replace the big private banks. Finance might then finally be made to work for the benefit of society.

Belloc believed much of modern wealth was an illusion. The real standard of living in pre-capitalist societies was higher than generally understood; the extra wealth generated by capitalism much overstated. Illusory wealth was caused by a rotten financial system. The problem was 'usury' which meant *the taking of any interest whatever upon an unproductive loan.* Such loans were not backed by real wealth. War loans, made for purely destructive purposes, were the ultimate example. In traditional societies it was up to the lender to make sure that a loan could legitimately carry interest. This was impossible in a modern financial system, with so many intermediaries between lender and borrower. Belloc's views on usury reflected anti-semitic prejudice on top of traditional church teaching. Usury was both a sin and a disease, eating away at the vitals of the economy:

a claim for an increase of wealth which is not really
present at all … [it] must progressively soak up the
wealth which men produce into the hands of those
who lend money.

By the end of *Economics for Helen* these different
forms of illusory wealth seem almost as big a threat as a
'Servile State'.

The slumps of the inter-war period led to mass un-
employment. Many believed that a sort of black hole
must exist at the heart of capitalism. The sums just didn't
'add up'. There was too little demand in the economy be-
cause workers were paid too little. Belloc agreed: capital-
ism *distributes less purchasing power than it creates*. When
goods were sold most of the takings went to capitalists,
who were more likely to save the money or to spend it
on period houses, antiques etc. that created no employ-
ment. This led to a constant scramble for new markets, to
plug the gap in demand for factory output. Such 'under-
consumption' theories attracted many converts (notably
Ezra Pound). In real life Belloc was never one for under-
consumption – a man of reckless generosity, forever ply-
ing his friends with champagne. They must have smiled
to read that champagne was an 'economic imaginary' par
excellence:

> created by the silly person who is willing to pay
> from a pound to thirty shillings for a thing worth
> two shillings and sixpence…

Be that as it might, Belloc believed that much modern wealth was really a form of double counting. *Economics for Helen* ends with a warning that governments were trying to tax wealth which did not exist:

> And this is probably the main reason why so many highly developed societies have broken down towards the end of their brilliance through the demands of their tax-gatherers who worked on assessments inflated out of all reality by a mass of economic imaginaries.

In 1936 Belloc published *The Restoration of Property*, a manifesto for a 'Distributist' State. It was to be a society of small family enterprises. Property ownership, especially of the means of production, would be spread as widely as possible. Belloc held out little hope of success but it was important to try because:

> failing such a change, our industrial society must necessarily end in the restoration of slavery.

Distributists were in two minds about competition. In principle, it would prevent the growth of harmful monopolies. In practice, competitive markets were a playground for the unscrupulous, tending inevitably to concentrate wealth in a few private hands. Most businessmen did all they could to stifle competition,* using stratagems

---

* The idea has a respectable pedigree. Much as Adam Smith disliked the meddling of governments and their pointless wars, he could also be scathing about the business community – 'an order of men whose inter-

that ran from relatively benign to distinctly sinister. Large businesses could spread their overhead costs more widely. They could hire the best brains, fund expensive research and monopolise information. They could afford massive advertising and PR campaigns. They had the cash-flow to finance their own expansion, and the ear of the banks if more was needed. They could unleash price-wars on upstart competitors. They could buy political favours and influence the laws. And if all else failed, they could abuse the legal system with costly litigation. Belloc suggested ways to redress the odds in all these areas.

To preserve small shops, for example, Belloc wanted to handicap large chain stores with extra taxes and licences. Likewise, the big 'pub chains' were to be discouraged by every means. Money raised from the big fish should subsidise the minnows. Craftsmen should be organised in guilds, protected by charter, and helped to compete against factory-made goods. None of this was cheap or efficient. It was a 'luxury' but one that would be of immense benefit, socially, morally, even æsthetically. There was a reason why people put up with mass-produced tat:

> Men take what is imposed upon them and not what they themselves choose. Supply controls demand and not demand supply.

est is never exactly the same with that of the public, who have generally an interest to deceive and even to oppress the public, and who accordingly have, upon many occasions, both deceived and oppressed it...'

Some goods had to be mass-produced but many did not. Flour milling, for example, had fallen under the control of a few big firms during the wartime drive for cheapness. There was no need to mill flour in huge factories. With the right mix of 'differential tax' and subsidy, the local miller could thrive again. As for brewing:

> Better beer and a greater choice would result from penalising the large brewery and with the revenue subsidising the small one, down to the cottage brewer.

Craft beer has since become a commercial hit. Small brewers have flourished thanks to a consumer rebellion against dull beer, rather than any system of controls. Belloc underestimated the responsiveness of markets. On the other hand big brewing chains often buy up the challengers, as Belloc foresaw. He believed that big business would inevitably claw back its dominant position unless prevented by policy. He particularly loathed industrial takeovers, often the work of financiers using stock market manipulation to win control of vast empires. He would be dismayed by the growth of 'private equity', which controls an ever larger share of the economy through secretive structures owing little obligation towards the wider community. All forms of predatory financial engineering would be stopped under Distributism, through a mixture of regulation and taxation. The State would systematically favour smaller units over large ones. Where large enterprises were unavoidable, their shares would be widely owned, in penny packets.

Above all, Distributism meant getting land into as many hands as possible. Townsfolk should own their own houses. Leaseholders should own their freeholds. In the country small peasant farm holdings should be the norm. The aim was not more output or profit but as many viable smallholdings as possible, on which families could make a modest but independent living. Farmers should start by supplying their own table – cash crops came second (Belloc would deplore the sight of farmers getting their food from the supermarket). Smallholders should form cooperatives to market their produce. Special cooperative banks should look after farmers – all too often, their land was mortgaged to some city financier. The law should make it hard for big farmers to buy land from smaller ones; and much easier in the other direction. Peasants, as Belloc was happy to call them, should also be spared by the taxman:

> when you are attempting to re-establish a peasant-
> ry under adverse conditions, that peasantry must
> be privileged as against the diseased society around
> it.

As a libertarian, Belloc was not happy. This pro-gramme would need government interference on a grand scale. But a 'Servile State' was the greater evil. Capitalism had usurped the powers of the State in order to create *servile conditions*: to restore freedom, the same methods would have to be used against capitalism. However, it was no use looking to Parliament:

> Parliaments have everywhere proved irreconcilable with democracy. They are not the people. They are oligarchies, and these oligarchies are corrupt … They are in reality and can only be, cliques of professional politicians … Parliaments are necessarily the organs of plutocracy .

Belloc never forgot or forgave the failure of his parliamentary career. He thought parliamentary democracy might somehow give way to a system of chartered guilds, existing under a form of monarchy, but made no attempt to explain how this would happen or how it would work. His political and economic writing could be perfunctory, petulant, or worse. He was also given to anti-semitic outbursts. No one would take Belloc for a guide in any general sense. Yet one or two of his insights still feel uncomfortably relevant.

Five years after *Economics for Helen*, with its apocalyptic warnings about finance, a crash on Wall Street triggered the Great Depression. The slump became global and set the scene for the Second World War. It would be comforting to ignore Belloc as a crank obsessed with usury. But he surely has a point that loans given for 'unproductive purposes' carry financial risks – whether or not they are sinful. Private banks have the power to create purchasing power at will. It turned out, after the great crash of 2007-2008, that much of this had gone to fund exotic ventures in financial engineering; and that much of it was worthless. The house of cards has been growing again. Next time it collapses the damage will be spectacular.

Belloc was a man of the 1930s with a political agenda to match. As he frankly admitted, he was after a *reactionary revolution*. But it would rash to ignore the *Servile State*, with its warnings of a toxic alliance between State and business. Modern-day China or Russia are the most glaring but not the only examples. Even in mature democracies, the tools of 'State capture' have grown too strong for comfort. Business lobbyists are stronger, better prepared and far better funded than the politicians they seek to influence. All too often the agenda is set by a handful of media tycoons. Today's Big Data would horrify Belloc who warned as long ago as the 1930s about corporate control of information.

Finally, Belloc put a spotlight on economic insecurity. It remains a blight on the lives of millions. A third of adults in the UK have less than £600 in savings, a tenth, no savings at all. On top of this comes the insecurity of zero-hours contracts or short term tenancies. Insecurity is sometimes seen as a spur to effort. Belloc saw it as a driver of political and economic instability (a belief shared with J. K. Galbraith, who showed, in *The Affluent Society*, that modern business relies on maximum planning certainty, and that 'insecurity is something that is cherished only for others'). Belloc was surely right about insecurity. Globalised markets powered by a heedless financial system have left many communities feeling impoverished, powerless and resentful. The political consequences are all too plain. One need not share Belloc's agenda (property ownership as an alternative to State provision) to agree that a wider distribution of property would give people more of a stake in the system, a feeling of greater control, more reason to support the liberal order. To be fully part of society people need at least some assets of their own. To quote Sir Francis Bacon – perhaps a Distributist ahead of his time:

Money is like muck, not good except it be spread.

EZRA POUND

1885-1972

THERE died a myriad,
And of the best, among them,
For an old bitch gone in the teeth,
For a botched civilisation.

HUGH SELWYN MAUBERLEY

Ezra Pound spent the First World War in London. As an American, he was not called up to fight. But few of his fellow artists were spared. He was much affected by the loss of his great friend the sculptor Henri Gaudier -Brzeska.* He came to believe that a rotten financial system had caused the war, allowing profiteers to fatten while the best went out to die. In 1919 he met Major C. H. Douglas, a military engineer whose 'Social Credit'† theory had caught the attention of the literary avant-

---

* Gaudier Brzeska's drawing of Pound can be seen in the Kettle's Yard collection at Cambridge. It was a preparatory drawing for a bust which became Pound's most treasured possession (now NGA, Washington).
† Not to be confused with the Chinese Government's version of 'Social Credit', a system for evaluating the social, political and financial 'health' of every citizen in the land.

garde. It was the start of a life-long crusade against the evils of 'finance'. Pound became obsessed with economics, to the point of writing a primer on the subject, the *ABC of Economics* (1933).

A brief outline of Social Credit may help as it looms so large in Pound's life. While working in an aircraft factory during the First World War, Major Douglas noticed that the sums paid out as wages, salaries and dividends came to much less than the total price of factory output. He found this was true of all factories, which led to an alarming conclusion: the community's income was not enough to buy what it collectively produced. The gap was filled by the banks, with loans which then had to be repaid. To keep going, the system had to keep growing. This led to ever greater waste, as production was geared to the logic of the financial system instead of people's real needs. It also led to a constant war for new markets, leading eventually to real wars, notably the First World War:

> the sum of the wages, salaries and dividends, distributed in respect of the world's total production will buy an ever decreasing fraction of it, and can never control it.

The traditional 'factors of production' are land, labour and capital. In essence Douglas added a fourth – the 'cultural heritage'. This represented all the past knowledge and infrastructure embodied in the productive process – roads and bridges, education, accumulated scientific knowledge. In Douglas's system, this cultural heritage would earn a dividend for its rightful owners, the public, to make up the gap in their purchasing power. At the same time, Social Credit would eliminate the waste at the heart of capitalism by steering credit into 'socially necessary' production. This would meet the real needs of the community, while consuming far less labour and resources

Douglas thought money had lost its traditional function as a 'store of value' and a 'medium of exchange' and had become a tool for the enrichment of financiers. Running the monetary system was a job for the community, not privately owned banks. Money should be a sort of ration card: a 'ticket' or 'token'. Enough 'tickets' should be issued to absorb all 'socially necessary' production. People would be paid according to their productivity, or 'time energy units'; and receive extra tickets as a 'national dividend' based on a share of the 'cultural heritage'. Investment, credit and prices would all be administered through a public 'Credit Agency'.

Douglas was a crank who later drifted into anti-semitism. His Social Credit would have been a bureaucratic nightmare. But he had stumbled on a real problem. Say's Law, one of the oldest in economics, said there was always enough demand in the system to buy what was produced (because all costs of production were paid out as wages, dividends, profits etc.). Accordingly, the economic slump was not supposed to exist and orthodox economists had no cure for it. Keynes showed that Say's Law can take a long time to operate and that governments might sometimes need to 'over-spend' in the meantime, to compensate for a shortfall in private-sector demand. While Keynes had no time for Social Credit, he did allow that:

> Major Douglas is entitled to claim as against some of his orthodox adversaries, that he at least has not been wholly oblivious of the outstanding problem of our economic system … A private perhaps, but not a major, in the braver army of heretics … who, following their intuitions, have preferred to see the truth obscurely and imperfectly, rather than to maintain error, reached indeed with clearness and consistency and by easy logic, but on hypotheses inappropriate to the facts.
>
> *General Theory*, 1936

Pound was a believer from the start. Reviewing Douglas's *Economic Democracy* in 1920 he hailed:

> A genius as valid in its own speciality as anything we can point to in the arts.

Pound did however see that Social Credit might be hard to put into practice. Another review from the same year ended on a quizzical note:

> we are to be saved by a few hundred chartered but honest accountants working in a plate-glass room under communal supervision, which, if we are,

alas! destined for salvation despite our natural in-
clinations, may be as good a method as any.

A decade later, all doubt had gone. In 1924 Pound
moved to Italy, where he came to admire Mussolini's Fas-
cist regime. While most of Europe and the USA grappled
with the Great Depression, Italy enjoyed relative eco-
nomic calm. Mussolini mobilised the country's resources
on a grand scale. He drained the Pontine marshes, a vast
malarial swamp, and turned them into fertile farms. He
built Europe's first motorway. A promise of full employ-
ment hid the more brutal underside of a police state. It all
seemed to show that conventional wisdom was bankrupt.
Pound became a strident supporter of Social Credit.

Rapallo, a small coastal resort near Genoa, became
Pound's base until the end of the Second World War.
Distance from the literary centres of London and Paris
seemed to broaden his ambition. He embarked on the
Cantos, a sprawling poetic universe that would emerge
over the next forty years. It ranged from ancient China
to modern Europe, from heaven to hell, from the gods
to the gold standard, banking, and even factory finance.
There was also a stream of articles, letters, pamphlets and
broadcasts. Pound called his economics 'Volitionist' – an
economics of the will. It was a blend of Major Douglas,
Mussolini, and the evils of banking, all summed up in the
ABC of Economics which appeared in 1933. It begins with
a flourish:

The aim of this brochure is to express the funda-

mentals of economics so simply and clearly that
even people of different economic schools and fac-
tions will be able to understand each other when
they discuss them.

Pound took it as a given that production was 'solved'. The
main problem in economics was distribution:

There are enough goods, there is superabundant
capacity to produce goods in superabundance.
Why should anyone starve?

The answer was that nobody would starve if the money, or
'tokens', were properly distributed. The tokens should go to
those who invented things, made them, grew them, trans-
ported or mended them. But too many who wanted such
work could find none; while too many tokens ended up in
the pockets of the unproductive:

Someone else has got all the tokens; or someone
else has done all the work 'needed'.

People had a right to work and to some basic economic
security. The work should be shared out (as Shelley had
proposed 120 years earlier). A fairer distribution of 'tokens'
– or 'certificates' – would increase demand because the poor
were more likely to spend all they earned. But there was still
a basic problem of too little demand, as explained by a 'hard
headed Scotsman' (i.e. Douglas):

an increasingly large proportion of goods pro-
duced never gets its certificate. Some fool or some

skunk plays mean … We artists have known this
for a long time, and laughed. We took it as our
punishment for being artists.

In the *ABC of Economics* Pound tried to explain why
the system produces too little purchasing power to absorb
what it produces. He made a shorter job of it in Can-
to XXXVIII where he explains *the financial aspect* of a
factory:

> What it pays in wages and dividends
> stays fluid, as power to buy, and this power is less
> per forza, damn blast your intellex, is less
> than the total payments made by the factory
> (as wages, dividends AND payments for raw
>   material
> bank charges, etcetera)
> and all, that is the whole, that is the total
> of these is added into the total of prices
> caused by that factory, any damn factory
> and there is and must be therefore a clog
> and the purchase can never
> (under the present system) catch up with
> prices at large.

The solution lay in providing *honest certificates of work
done*. Pound does not say how this would happen but it
would be the central problem of economics. He seems
to have realised that replacing the market system with an
administrative one might have drawbacks:

you must still have constant caginess not to find yourself in October with nothing but wheat or nothing but aluminium frying pans.

And towards this end there is probably no equation other than the greatest watchfulness of the greatest number of the most competent.

Social Credit came with radical views on money. If it was a 'ticket', corresponding to a share in total output, it followed that it should be linked to that output, not to the amount of gold in the vaults. Most experts believed in the 'gold standard'. The value of the currency, expressed in gold, had to be kept constant. If that meant wage cuts or job losses, so be it. Workers who resisted such cuts were said to be 'pricing themselves out of a job'. Pound thought this absurd: the currency was there to serve the community. He pleaded for *controlled inflation… more certificates must be granted when more goods are produced.* In other words, the amount of currency in circulation should grow in line with production, leaving headroom for further growth (but avoiding inflation, which would happen if the money supply grew too quickly). Pound was on to something: most currencies are now managed with a view to full employment and growth, as well as relative price stability.

More fundamentally, Pound said that money was a public good, depending on trust, the legal system and a well-functioning social order. It was also a ration card which gave people a right to a share in total output. As such, it should be managed by and for the community. It was perverse to let private banks create almost all the money in the economy; and absurd that the State should have to pay the banks to borrow 'tickets'. There was no need to pay interest on the public debt. The State should *lend, not borrow*, nor should it need to levy taxes to finance public spending:

> I take it that in the perfect economic state the cost of money is reduced to nothing, to something like the mere cost of postage, and that this cost is borne by the State i.e. Distributed so as to be a burden to no one in particular.
>
> The moment you conceive money as certificates of work done, taxes are an anomaly, for it would be perfectly simple to issue such certificates of work done for the State, without wasting effort in re-collecting certificates already in circulation

There are echoes of these ideas in Modern Monetary Theory (MMT). Like Pound, supporters of MMT think the State does not need taxes to pay for its spending (taxes are there to reduce demand for real resources, so as to leave room for the needs of the State – otherwise there could be inflation). Like Pound, MMT sees no need to pay interest on the Government debt (though the State may choose to do so, to keep control of interest rates in the rest of the economy). MMT is a hotly contested

theory but, faced with a mountain of bills, some govern-
ments seem to be drifting towards it.

Pound also fell under the influence of Silvio Gesell,
a German businessman-cum-anarchist. Gesell believed
that all land should belong to the community and be
leased out to those best able to use it, irrespective of
country, race or creed. 'Free Land' found few takers
but 'Free Money', its financial twin, attracted much at-
tention. Gesell believed that money exaggerated both
booms and busts. It was hoarded in difficult times,
just when it should be put to work; it flowed too freely
when times were good, leading to speculative excess. If
money was less easy to hoard it would perform its other
functions better. Gesell proposed a new form of money
that would steadily lose value. Stamps would have to
be affixed to keep banknotes in circulation, for example
1p weekly on a £10 note or just over 5% annually. This
would discourage excessive saving and drive money into
productive use. The idea received support from some
prominent economists, such as Irving Fisher of Yale. It
was also put into practice in the Austrian town of Wörgl
– an episode described in Canto LXXIV:

> … and when a note of the
> small town of Wörgl went over
> a counter in Innsbruck
> and the banker saw it go over
> all the slobs in Europe were terrified.

There were the plenty of flaws in the scheme but Gesell had seen that people hoard cash in difficult times, which can lead to a slump in demand and make a depression worse. Pound soon added Gesell's depreciating money to his magic mix. He would presumably welcome today's negative interest rates, introduced at a time of crisis to avoid a repeat of the Great Depression. But he would surely regret their side-effect of deeper inequality, as the extra money has puffed up the price of existing assets, owned by those who are already well off.

The economic misery of the 1930s was a scandal, unnecessary and unjust. Pound began with good intentions:

> When the total nation hasn't... enough food for its people, that nation is poor. When enough food exists and people cannot get it by honest labour, the State is rotten ...
>
> It is the business of the STATE to see that there is enough money in the hands of the WHOLE people, and in adequately rapid EXCHANGE, to effect distribution of all wealth produced and producible ... Until every member of the nation eats three times a day and has shelter and clothing, a nation is either lazy or unhealthy.
>
> *What is Money for?*, 1939

Pound's anger was understandable and widely shared. An answer came after the war, with the Welfare State (though many still do not *eat three times a day*). But

Pound was impatient. Anger hardened into obsession. He embarked on a crusade against 'usury', the age-old scapegoat. Canto XLV is a tirade on usury which ends:

> Usura slayeth the child in the womb
> It stayeth the young man's courting
> It hath brought palsey to bed, lyeth
> between the young bride and her bridegroom
> CONTRA NATURAM
> They have brought whores for Eleusis
> Corpses are set to banquet
> At behest of usura.

> N.B. Usury: A charge for the use of purchasing power, levied without regard to production; often without regard to the possibilities of production.

Usury was the devil and banks the fallen angels, notably the Bank of England. Pound often reminded his readers that it was still (until 1946) a private company. A prospectus put out by the Bank's founder, Sir William Paterson, in 1694 provides material for Canto XLVI:

> Said Paterson:
> Hath benefit of interest on all the moneys
> which it, the bank, creates out of nothing

The Banca Di San Giorgio in Genoa was another *hell bank* set up purely to make money. In spreading the spirit of usury, it had poisoned the wells of culture. It was no accident, in Pound's view that that Genoa had produced no art of any consequence and played little part in the Renaissance. There was at least one good bank, the Monte Dei Paschi of Siena,* founded in 1472. Pound spent weeks in the archives researching its history, in preparation for a group of Cantos on banks good and bad. It begins with Canto XLII which celebrates the Monte:

> FIXED in the soul, nell'anima, of the Illustrious
>   College,
> They had been ten years proposing such a Monte,
> That is, a species of bank.

The Monte was virtuous because it was backed by productive grazing lands, a natural source of wealth. Its growth had to respect limits set by nature. It was sustainable, its profits were limited by statute and its aim was the public good:

> And the lesson is the very basis of solid banking. The CREDIT rests in ultimate on the ABUN-DANCE OF NATURE , on the growing grass that can nourish the living sheep.
> And the moral is in the INTENTION. It was not for the conqueror's immediate short-sighted profit, but to restart the life and productivity of Siena that this bank was contrived.
>
> *Social Credit: An Impact,* 1935

* No bank stays virtuous for ever. The Monte almost went under in a series of monumental scandals that erupted in 2013.

Pound had no interest in material goods. So long as he had books and writing materials he was content. He looked forward happily to the end of economic growth:

> it was indeed a bright day when some ruler per-
> ceived that there was a limit to the dimension
> quantity in the nation's productivity, I mean a
> limit to the quantity of production that could be
> advantageous either to a given nation or to the
> world, but that there is no limit to the dimension
> quality ... In the dimension QUALITY there is
> ample field for all human energy.
>
> *ABC of Economics*

A stationary economy must have seemed natural to a man steeped in the Chinese classics. Cantos LII-LXI take the reader back to China's ancient past, presented by Pound as a time of order, harmony and respect for nature's laws. Confucius preached order based on discipline within the self, within the family and so on up to the Emperor; the rites and customs to be respected at each level; the whole in harmony with nature. Pound was first and foremost a poet, his aims were aesthetic: to rescue 'the beautiful' from the market place and restore the eternal verities. In turning to Confucius, Pound turned his back on the waste, ugliness and greed of the modern world. But he overlooked the slavery, poverty and violence of the ancients. His arcadia, a place of austere simplicity, might work as poetry. He believed in it as a programme for action; and when it fell on deaf ears in Washington he took a tragic turn towards the forces of darkness.

Though he settled in Europe, Pound cared deeply about America. There had been a chance to build a healthy society in the new world. Instead it was repeating, even magnifying, the faults of the old. American history was an epic struggle against financial manipulators who used a *false system of book-keeping* to rob the plain honest folk, the small farmers, the workers, the men who turned out to fight for American independence. The heroes were Adams and Jefferson (the second and third Presidents) who wanted to spare the USA from a financial system on the British model. The ultimate villain was Alexander Hamilton, now the subject of a hit musical but according to Canto LXII *the prime snot in ALL American history*. Pound devoted a series of Cantos to this primordial battle.

During the war of independence the American colonies issued credit notes to pay and equip their forces. These became almost worthless after the war and were mostly picked up by speculators. In the meantime the 13 colonies had become the USA. Hamilton, as the first US Treasury Secretary, insisted that the US Government should repay the colonies' debts in full. The speculators made a killing but from then on the US Government was able to borrow freely in times of need. For Pound, the *scandal of the Assumption* opened the way to a banking system on the British model, with all the associated speculation and financial trickery. It was America's original sin:

> Usury ruined the Republic
>> *Economic Nature of the United States*, 1944

One might expect Pound to support President Roosevelt's New Deal, a massive programme of public works that lifted America out of the Great Depression. Instead he attacked the New Deal, because the money had been raised on Wall Street, creating vast debts for posterity. If the Administration had paid for the New Deal with Gesell's depreciating money, they could have cleared the debt within a few years. Pound bombarded US Senators with advice, all in vain. Disappointment with his country of birth blinded him to the evil afoot in his adopted one. He spent the Second World War in Italy, pursuing his obsessions. Attacks on 'usury' merged disastrously with anti-semitism. As if the war were a side-show, he recast Mussolini, and even Hitler, as actors in his own monetary epic:

> USURY is the cancer of the world, which only the surgeon's knife of Fascism can cut out of the life of nations.
>> *What is Money For?*, 1939

> This war is no whim of Mussolini's, nor of Hitler's. This war is a chapter in the long and bloody

tragedy which began with the foundation of the
Bank of England in far-away 1694.

Gold and Work, 1944

When Pound wrote the second of these extracts he
was wanted for high treason, over his broadcasts on the
Fascist radio. Before long, advancing US forces arrested
and locked him in a metal cage (where he wrote the *Pisan
Cantos*). The charges were eventually dropped, but only
after he spent twelve years in a mental hospital, a stay that
probably saved him from the electric chair. At the start of
The ABC of Economics he declared: *I shall have no peace
until I get the subject off my chest.* Peace was forty years
in coming. Towards the end, his views began to soften.
Looking back, shortly before his death in 1972, he wrote:

RE USURY:
I was out of focus, taking a symptom for a cause.
The cause is AVARICE.

In 1944, when Pound was led away to his cage, May-
nard Keynes was in the USA planning the post-war eco-
nomic order: the IMF, the World Bank and the policies
that would deliver thirty years of growth. Economics had
finally come up with some answers.The days were over
when a poet could rewrite the text books. Pound had
tested the genre to destruction. For better or for worse,
poetry and economics now went their separate ways.

FURTHER READING

It feels presumptuous to recommend further reading in such well-trodden fields as poetry and economics. This book is about the small furrow where the two intersect. Some of the literature about this is fairly academic. Here are a few works that I found useful, and that might interest a busy general reader.

James Buchan, *Frozen Desire* (Macmillan, 1998) Not cited in my book but a most readable and engaging meditation on money through the ages, with a wealth of cultural references.

Karl Polanyi, *The Great Transformation* (1944). More detail on pp. 87-8. Not poetry but a great example of the humanities throwing light on economic problems (and history has its own muse, Clio). In the Beacon Press (2001) edition, a foreword by the famous economist Joseph Stiglitz makes a powerful link between Polanyi's book and present-day problems.

Colin Campbell, *The Romantic Ethic and the Spirit of Modern Consumerism* (Blackwell, 1987). More detail on p. 137n. Now hard to find (except as a Kindle

book). At the scholarly end of the spectrum but well
worth the effort.

Raymond Williams, *Culture and Society 1780-1950* (1958).
Hugely influential study of the interplay between cul-
ture and the industrial revolution (written from a left-
wing perspective).

Donald Winch, *Riches and Poverty: an intellectual history
of political economy in Britain 1750-1834* (CUP, 1996).
At the academic end of the spectrum and confined to
the earlier period. But worth the effort.

For more context, a short history of economics might
help. See Robert Heilbroner *The Wordly Philosophers* (7th
ed. 1999, Touchstone); or Niall Kishtainy *A Little History
of Economics* (Yale 2017): reminders that economics is not
a monolith or its 'laws' eternal.

Another way to approach economics is through
a good biography. For Adam Smith, try Jesse Norman
(*Adam Smith: What he Thought and Why it Matters,* Pen-
guin 2019) or James Buchan (*The Authentic Adam Smith:
His Life and Ideas*, Atlas Books, 2006).

In their contribution to the *Cambridge Companion to
Adam Smith*, Amartya Sen and Emma Rothschild, pro-
vide a wonderful antidote to clichés about Adam Smith
(Sen, like Smith, is a great economist equally at home
in philosophy; a profoundly humane thinker whose *On
Economics and Ethics* seeks to reconnect the two).

For Keynes, Robert Skidelsky's three-volume biography is a classic.

J. K. Galbraith is always a good read. *The Great Crash, 1929* (most recent edition Penguin, 2009) is short and sadly topical. Very unusually for an economist, he also wrote novels. *A Tenured Professor* (Mariner Books, 2001) is a delight.

Some of today's economists clearly feel that their subject has become too narrow and needs to reconnect with the humanities, just as the poets felt. The Introduction (p. 15) cites two distinguished examples:

Esther Duflo and Abhijit Banerjee, *Good Economics for Hard Times* (Penguin, 2019)

Robert Skidelsky, *What's Wrong with Economics* (Yale, 2021)

Another recent book, well worth reading (by Joe Earle, Cahal Moran and Zach Ward-Perkins, *The Econocracy*, Penguin, 2017) is subtitled 'On the Perils of Leaving Economics to the Experts'....

ACKNOWLEDGEMENTS

I first thought of this book during a spell of sick leave over thirty years ago, since when it has progressed in (long) stops and occasional starts. Jane, my wife, to whom this book is dedicated, has given wise and patient counsel throughout.

Jane introduced me to that great polymath the late Dr. Richard Luckett, Pepys Librarian at Magdalene College Cambridge, who put me onto *Economics for Helen* and even gave me a copy.

Many thanks to the British Library and its staff, where much of the reading was done (some of it in the old British Museum Reading Room of fond memory).

Alexander Fyjis-Walker at Pallas Athene has published a stable of books on similar themes, especially on Ruskin. I am most grateful to him for taking this one on.

The transition from reclusive scribbler to brazen self-promoter is not easy. Many thanks to Martha Halford-Fumagalli for guiding me through the PR jungle.

And finally, a big thank you to my daughter Isobel for providing the perspective of a younger reader (and a fine eye for typos).

INDEX

208; on US monetary system 209; and fascism 13,199, 210
WORKS: *ABC of Economics* 7, 196ff; *The Cantos* 199, 201, 204-7; *Social Credit: An Impact* 208; *What is Money for?* 205, 210; *Gold and Work* 211

power imbalance: defect of supply and demand 86, 130, 183; Belloc on 183

rational economic man 37, 125, 178

rent (unearned income): Shelley on 54, 55; Ricardo's theory of 118-20; Shaw on 165, 174; weakens 'life force' 174

Rerum Novarum 153

rhinoceros (price of) 112

Ricardo, David: and classical economics 9; and *Confessions of an English Opium Eater* 107-8; De Quincey elaborates his theories 110ff; labour theory of value 110, 131-2; R's theory of rent 118-20; Ricardian vice 119, 132; *Principles of Political Economy and Taxation* 110, 118, 131

Ruskin, John 8, 10, 14; division of labour 124; political economy (mass delusion) 125; price of

labour 126ff; on skills and duties of businessman 127; nature of wealth 133-5; 'illth' 133; green economics and market failure 135-6; money, gold and usury 137-8; guilds and corporate society 139-43
WORKS *Munera Pulveris* 10, 137-9; *Modern Painters* 123; *The Stones of Venice* 123; *The Nature of Gothic* 124-5; *Unto this Last* 125ff; *The Crown of Wild Olive* 135; *Time and Tide* 139-42; *Fors Clavigera* 142-3

Ruskin College, Oxford 144

Say's Law 197-8

Schumpeter, Joseph: *Capitalism, Socialism and Democracy* 77 n.

Scott, Sir Walter: 13-15; saves the Scottish Pound 7, 89ff; bankruptcy 90, on Scottish banking system: solid 93-4, social benefits of,95-6, helps regional revival 96-97; on utility 99; meets Adam Smith 100-2
WORKS: *Rob Roy* 89; *Letters of Malachi Malagrowther* 90-102; *Journal* 90, 91, 97-8, 105

Scott, (Lady) Charlotte 105

Shaw, George Bernard: co-founds LSE 8, 178; on

After reading history & economics at Cambridge and two years in a merchant bank, John Ramsden joined the Foreign and Commonwealth Office in 1975. He was posted in Dakar and Vienna, and then spent two years in Hanoi (chronicled in *Hanoi After the War,* Skira 2017). He spent the rest of his career in Europe, including a secondment to the Treasury and posts in Berlin (1990-93), the UN in Geneva and Croatia (as Ambassador from 2004-2008). He has also written *The Box in the Attic*, based on letters from relatives who took part in some of the great events of the last century.